LETTERS
to the
BROKENHEARTED

**Woman to Woman Advice on
Refocusing, Rebuilding, and Reloving**

PAMELA A. LARDE, PH.D.

Tandem Light Press
LAWRENCEVILLE, GA

LETTERS TO THE BROKENHEARTED
Copyright © 2013 by Pamela A. Larde

Published in the United States by Tandem Light Press
Lawrenceville, GA 30044
www.tandemlightpress.com

First printing, February 2013
Second printing, September 2021

Music lyrics and poetry used with permission.

Library of Congress Cataloging-in-Publication Data:

Larde, Pamela A.
Letters to the brokenhearted / Pamela A. Larde
p. cm.
ISBN 987-1-7353210-2-8 (hardcover)
2013930050
Second Edition

In the description of some of her personal life experiences, the author has
recreated events, locations, and conversations from her memories of them. In
some instances, in order to maintain anonymity, she has used pseudonyms.

10 9 8 7 6 5 4

Printed in the United States of America
Book design by Tandem Light Press
Set in Cambria
Edited by Tim Morrison & Caroline Smith
Author photo by Steve Pelosi Photography

For my sisters who just want to smile again

CONTENTS

CONTENTS

ACKNOWLEDGMENTS

Thank you, from the bottom of my heart to the following people who provided the love, guidance, and support needed to make this work possible:

Alfonso and Georgia Larde, my parents, the two people who nurtured this creative passion of mine from the very first moment I discovered the written word. You guys have made all of this completely possible for me by laying a strong foundation for my life in my early years and for hanging in my corner through the good, the bad, and the ugly.

My son and daughter, who got used to mom sitting at the computer during all hours of the day and night and who always gave me a reason to keep pressing forward through each challenge over the years.

My uplifters and sister friends, Michelle Mendoza and Carla Fullwood, who reminded me that the best way to get over a broken heart is to do what I do best...write it out.

My extended family and friends who have stood as pillars in my corner through each of my challenges and became my greatest cheerleaders as I poured my heart into this book, but specifically: Dewayne Larde, Wendy Cole, Victor Glover, Natasha Copeland, LaKesha Russ, A'Nette Knox, and J'Nette Knox.

My mentor, Dr. John L. Hoffman, who has relentlessly supported and inspired me, and has never stopped believing in me.

The many supporters who contributed to the funding of this book.

My publishing team: Dr. Tim Morrison & Caroline Smith, my editors who kept me on my toes with their strict, no-nonsense feedback; the Booklogix team, who took care of finishing touches, editing, and printing, and the Peachtree Corners Barnes and Noble writing group that provided invaluable feedback as I trudged along; Marlon Hines, my highly talented original book cover designer; and an absolutely amazing public relations crew consisting of my intern, Nicole Stroud, and Bee Season Consulting.

My exes, without whom the valuable lessons I've learned over the years would not be possible. I am grateful for all that you have done to make it possible for us to be on friendly terms today.

God bless each and every one of you.

Most importantly, I give thanks to my Lord and Savior Jesus Christ, whose love has carried me through each trial, and whose grace has allowed me to walk and live in peace.

PREFACE

The Art of Kintsugi: You Hold the Gold

There is a fine art to healing after a broken heart. The science is in the therapy many of us need. In the way our bodies respond to pain. In the renewed need for human connection. The art shows up in the myriad of ways that are lives are forever changed. The art is in how we learn to dance all over again. It is the new canvas of our lives waiting to be painted. It is in the creative ways we discover our strength to carry on. Heartbreak challenges us to accept what has been dismantled and to take what is left of us to rebuild and create something new.

Kintsugi is a Japanese art that beautifully illustrates the powerful transformation of going from heartbreak to healing. It is the craft of using gold to repair and rebuild broken pottery pieces that become repurposed art pieces that represent the beauty of renewal. Our broken pieces, our flaws, and our imperfections imbued with beauty and purpose, are worthy of being pieced together with gold. Kintsugi finds beauty in our scars and reminds us that the process of healing enables us to create an even greater, even more unique, even more beautiful, and a wildly more resilient version of ourselves.

The cover design of this book honors this 400+ year Japanese tradition and encourages us to delve deeply, not only into the science and psychology of healing, but also into the art, the emotion, and the creativity that brings the science to life. Our healing is in our hands. We hold the gold. What we create with our beautifully unique pieces is totally up to the artist. Allow the Kintsugi artist in you to refocus, rebuild, and relove your way to powerful, life-changing healing.

INTRODUCTION

When the time comes to transition out of one place, how you leave is how you will transition into the next.
Do your best to leave clean and with integrity.

- Melva L. Henderson
Pastor at World Outreach Church

The Unraveling

It was supposed to be my summer on cloud nine—a once in a lifetime celebration worthy of Jamaican cruises, trips to Europe, and dazzling new diamond rings. It was time to finally live it up and usher in this new chapter of my life. I had just graduated with my Ph.D., and I was ready to kick off my shoes and celebrate. I had overcome much to reach this point: juggling fulltime work with mom and wife duties, and staying on top of my coursework through pregnancy and childbirth. For years, I had tolerated the folks who told me that I shouldn't have been doing this, and I endured the disappointment of having a husband who discouraged me from pursuing the dream to begin with. It was with a bull-headed determination that I pressed on. *If I can have nothing else for myself, this I will have.* And that summer I finally did it.

I graduated with a fresh Kool-Aid smile on my face. I was that graduate who cha-cha'd across the stage, struck a few extra poses for the photographer, and thrust both arms in the air before skipping back to my seat. Little did I know, my whole world was about to come crashing down. That very day was to be the last great milestone worth celebrating in my marriage. There would be no cruises, no trips to Europe, no dazzling new diamonds, not even a romantic dinner on the town, because our big lie—the one we worked so hard to keep under wraps— chose *this* season to reveal itself to the world. Just weeks after I danced across that stage, I was backslapped with the reality that my marriage was finally over.

Instead of reeling over being done with school forever, I spent that summer caught in between what seemed to be perfect on the outside and the naked, dirty truth of what existed on the inside. My husband was cheating on me. That beautiful suburban home of ours was not quite as manicured as it had appeared to be. I couldn't run from it anymore. The life we had orchestrated was on the verge of shattering. It had been this way from the very beginning, but I tried with all my might to hold on. It wasn't until this particular summer—when the residue of his actions began to rise to the surface—that I was finally brave enough to let go. This time, it was our too-good-to-be-true, gorgeously coy neighbor who once lived across the street from us. The twenty-one-year-old's number popped up on his phone one morning, even though she had moved out of the neighborhood years ago and remained estranged from her family. I needed no explanation. This man was cheating on me. The small torch that still burned inside of me, holding on to hope that our marriage might still stand a chance, burned out on that very day.

There would be no more chances after this one. Each year since we had married, there was something—an old girlfriend texting flirtatious exchanges for Valentine's Day, or some random chick from one of those remote towns he traveled to on business who suddenly became a Facebook friend. There was always something, but never a trace of evidence—just some apparent illusion of mine. So on that hot morning in June, as I held his phone in my hand in silence, he swore that what I saw was just another illusion, that it wasn't what it seemed, and that our ex-neighbor had only called him to seek his help because she was hungry and homeless. My gut told me otherwise.

I was in a paralyzing state of limbo that summer. One phone call didn't seem grounds enough to walk away from eleven years of trying to make a bad-relationship-turned-marriage work. Still, I desperately wanted out of the cycle. I knew this wasn't just a phone call, but I couldn't walk away on what little I had.

For the next few months, I forced myself to get up every day, to be a wife and mother, to continue on with this life that I knew full well was a bald-faced lie. When I found moments alone, the tears flowed freely. I beat on my pillow, slammed dishes in the sink, and kicked myself for still being there. I felt trapped. Absolutely no one knew what was going on in my world because when I stepped out into the sun, I plastered on my smile and played the award-winning role of happy all-American wife.

By the end of that agonizing summer, the truth came out—as it often does. After I finally confronted him with a collection of phone bills decorated with rows and rows of the twenty-one-year-old's number, he admitted that the phone call in question was one of many encounters over the past three years. THREE years. Three years behind my back. Three years in my own neighborhood. Three years—and our daughter was only two. "I wanted to tell you, but I was afraid that you would leave me," is what he said. And he was right. A week after our fifth wedding anniversary, I boxed up my tears, packed up whatever my two arms could carry, and left those eleven years of heartache behind me, relieved that it was finally over. Because it all happened so quickly, I was unsure of what was to happen next in my life. I moved forward anyway, brokenhearted and betrayed, but relieved that I didn't have to try to figure all of this out anymore. It was over. I was free. But I had a whole lot of baggage to carry along with me.

When It's Time to Say Good-bye

Every brokenhearted person has her own story (I have three), and these stories may play out quite differently for each of us. I'm sure that if my ex wrote up his own version of our breakup story, it would be written quite differently. We all experience heartbreak in unique ways, but in the end, it just hurts like hell. Every woman reading this book will not have experienced infidelity, will not have been brokenhearted while married, may not have been the innocent party in the relationship, and may not even be a woman—guys, you're more than welcome to eavesdrop and apply this stuff, too! Our experiences leading up to the breakup will be different, but the turmoil, the fear, and the process of recovering feel the same. It hurts, and its hard work that no one wants to do.

Yet, there comes a point when you realize that it's senseless to entertain conversations about why you or your partner should stay, when it becomes screamingly clear that the two of you may never share a promising future together. Maybe the circle of trust is broken. Maybe one partner is far more invested than the other, or perhaps compatibility simply doesn't exist. The arguments and awkward silences become routine. The conflict between contempt and love creeps in. You desperately want them to just be that amazing person they used to be—or that you thought they could be—even though you know in your heart that this is now a far-fetched dream. And yet, you hang on anyway because the heartache and fear of letting go are far stronger than the headache of holding on. *If this thing actually ends, what else is there?*

Despite the unanswered questions, you take your fears, tuck them in your back pocket and decide to walk away— or maybe you were pushed away. No matter how you got here, you've found yourself standing in the shadows of hurt and have been charged with the task to move on. If you've picked up this book, chances are there's something in you (or someone who loves you) telling you to let go. You deserve more than a forced, abusive, or infidelity-ridden relationship.

Your ex may be a great person, and they may very well still love you, but all great people—even those who love one another—aren't necessarily meant to be *together*.

Letting go is not an easy process, but the benefits of taking this step greatly outweigh the consequences of going against what your heart is telling you to do. As scary and unsettling as the thought may be, someone will eventually have to put a stop to the cycle, and, regardless of who initiates the breakup, it is up to you to do what it takes to let go and move forward with your life. It will hurt. That, unfortunately, is part of the process. It is never easy to let go of a loved one, but believe me when I say that holding on will hurt even more.

It's important to understand that this book is not a step-by-step guide about how to break up, nor is it a bash your ex fest. This is all about *letting go* after it has become clear that the relationship should not be restored. At this crossroads, we essentially have two choices—to obsess over what we cannot have or to move forward and embrace the future that awaits us. Regardless of whether or not there are kids involved, if this was a marriage, or a short-lived relationship, if it is truly over it is essential to find a way to let go. Holding on and obsessing over what we no longer have is self-destructive and only serves to further hurt those kids and any loved ones who may be involved.

The letters you are about to read were written for the woman who has made the decision to let go and doesn't know where to begin. They can also help the woman who is torn with the decision of staying and going, as I challenge those of us who share this experience of heartbreak to look within to create a healthy life in love, relationships, and spirituality. This book is for the woman who wants to find a way to accept that the relationship is over, regardless of who initiated or caused the breakup. Most of all, this is for the woman who is looking for a strategy that will enable her to heal, stay strong, and take her life to the next level.

The possibilities for personal growth, new love, and pure joy are endless once we make the decision to let go of a story that no longer exists. When we accept that a relationship has run its course and become proactive about healing the heart, we put ourselves in a position to elevate our living. But in order to do that (whether that is a renewed sense of self, a better job, or a happy marriage), it is essential that we first do one small thing...let go and move forward!

Refocus. Rebuild. Relove.

This book is grounded in my personal philosophy that we are primarily responsible for our own actions and decisions. We can't control the actions and decisions of other people. When we experience a breakup, everything seems to be out of our control, especially when we have done everything in our power to get the relationship back and it still fails. My letters to you are organized into three sections: refocus, rebuild, and relove. Within each section are three chapters filled with strategies I've personally used to let go and move forward after the ending of my own relationships. Rather than resorting to hopelessness, despair, or obsession, the letters provide guidance for taking control by *refocusing* your energy on the strengths that exist in your life, *rebuilding* what has been damaged, and *reloving* with a new purpose. By the time you reach this point, you should be well armed with a plan that can take you from brokenhearted to fully empowered. If you are ready to take this journey, you are already on the right track, my sister. Let's get started!

CHAPTER ONE

LETTING GO

HOLD ON TIGHT
By Pamela A. Larde

I lift my eyes and stare honesty in her face.
The truth is you and I morphed into an illusion long ago—
A selfish collection of heart's desires and senseless mutations
Of something we never resembled,
Somehow combined to create a you and I
That could never exist.

I clutch my livelihood with fragile hands and pull it close,
I can't hold it all together if I am still holding on to you.
I need only to hold on to the truth.
So today I am going to hold on tight
And let you go.

Letter 1

BROKEN PROMISES
BROKEN DREAMS

My Sister,

It's over. It hurts like hell. And all you can do is think about what you wish you had. Not too many experiences suck the life out of you more than loving someone you simply cannot—or should not—have. I've been there. I've had my heart broken, and I've experienced disappointment, broken promises, and broken dreams on more occasions than I would wish upon my worst enemy. I blame it on my over-the-top idealistic approach to life, which can be a great quality if used correctly. But me? I've always been a hopeless romantic with very little patience, and this hasn't proven to be the greatest combination for my relationships. Too often, it has resulted in my futile attempts to make something work with someone I was never meant to be with. The result? Heartbreak.

My experience includes sitting on both ends of the breakup scenario. I have been the one who let go quite easily, and I also have been the one who has had to have my fingers *pried* away one by one before being dragged off kicking and screaming. I didn't always want to let go, but doing so was the best decision I could have made in each situation. In my letters to you, I will periodically refer to some of my own experiences, which include letting go when I couldn't understand why it had ended, and being in relationships that were so unhealthy, I needed to *claw* my way out just to get air. In all cases, whether or not I initiated the breakup, I had some letting go to do—letting go of someone I deeply loved, of friendships, of hopes and dreams, of my role as a wife, of an image I had worked hard to uphold, of my pride. Letting go is much deeper than simply saying good-bye to someone and never speaking to them again. It involves true soul-searching and deliberate action. It's a process that must be done *on purpose* if you expect to come out of it healthy and whole.

In this first letter, I'll give you a snapshot of three relationships I experienced in which I had to be deliberate about letting go. These relationships were as drastically different from one another as the men involved in each situation. I dealt with moving forward after the decline of all three relationships quite differently, depending on the dynamics that came into play, but ultimately, I followed a strategy of refocusing, rebuilding, and reloving to fully heal. As a result, I was able to be real with myself about what I did and did not need in my life and act accordingly. I kept my heart focused on caring for myself and my eyes glued to the future. In each case, I managed to let go, move forward, and take the quality of my life to an entirely new level.

Out of respect for the privacy of these three guys, I've given them different names. Though I've learned that they were not right for me, and though we went through some really rough times together, today I have a great deal of respect for each of them, as they have moved forward with their own lives, and, like me, have become better people as a result of the lessons learned while we were together. While your experiences may not be identical to mine, I suspect that you will be able to identify with *some* aspects of my story and apply the lessons I've learned to your own life. So here are my guys:

Brian

I was eighteen years old when I met Brian. I was a young, first-year college student who knew very little about love. Raised in a strict family with a father who wouldn't allow boyfriends left me unusually inexperienced, clueless, and naïve. Brian, on the other hand, was twenty-four years old and had just ended a five-year relationship with a fiancée he told me had cheated on him. He and I met only a month before the date that their wedding would've happened. Imagine the baggage there! But, of course, at that stage in my life, I had no idea what baggage was. And as if that wasn't enough, he compulsively lied to me—saying that he was a police officer when he was really a security guard; that he had his own apartment when, actually, he lived with his mother; and that he was over his ex when he was still secretly seeing her.

I was young and naïve and I believed every word that came out of his mouth. He was the man I lost my virginity to, so while I was fully aware that I wasn't in love, I was definitely attached. When I got pregnant right away, he accused me of sleeping around and even threatened to kill me one night as I desperately insisted that this child was his. That entire relationship was a rollercoaster ride through hell. But I held on tightly. I was convinced that because I had lost my virginity, and because I was pregnant, I needed to marry this man. There was no other option in my mind. I could not be a single mother, so I blazed through all of the red flags (his fake suicide attempts to keep me from leaving him, his bouts of jealousy, his violent outbursts, his continued tendency to lie), and I stuck to my guns. *I'm pregnant. We're getting married.* Thank God that never happened.

But we almost did get married. Just one year after we met, and one year after he was supposed to marry his ex, Brian and I were planning a wedding of our own. I was now a young mom who had stopped going to school, taken a job at a grocery store, and was on a waiting list for low-income housing. I say this not a criticism of anyone who needs these resources to survive, but to point out that I was quite a ways off from where I was headed before I met Brian. I had dreams of becoming a prominent CNN reporter, a talk show host, and a best-selling novelist on the side. I had been accepted to nearly every college I applied to, and I had an opportunity to play softball on a scholarship. All of that quickly and drastically changed during my time with Brian. The vast majority of my family and friends had long dismissed me as a lost cause.

Then something happened in me two months before we were set to walk down the aisle. Brian had one of his jealous outbursts after I received a "Merry Christmas" phone call from one of my good friends from high school. My friend, Victor, had been away at college (and was one of the few who hadn't yet given up on me). He was extremely disappointed when he heard that I was no longer in school. He reminded me of the life dreams I had always spoken of during our high school years. His words were like a mirror to my face, showing me an image of myself that I hadn't bothered to stop and look at since meeting Brian. I was shocked. He was right. *What was I doing?* So, that Christmas Eve, after this final outburst from Brian, after watching him throw all of our Christmas gifts onto the lawn while cursing me out, accusing me of cheating with Victor, and threatening suicide, I decided that it was over. I left him that night and never looked back.

I left him, but there was still much I had to let go of. I had to let go of my fear of being a single mom, my preoccupation of what people would think of me, my negative perception of myself, my fantasy of walking down the aisle in the big gorgeous wedding gown I had purchased, and a great big ego that didn't want to admit that I was wrong about this guy. I also had a lot of other work to do. I needed to get back into school and get back on the track I was on before I decided to take that crazy detour. It was time for me to refocus, rebuild, and relove.

Jackson

My relationship with Jackson is the one that actually did result in marriage. I met Jackson in college a little over a year after leaving Brian. My son was almost two years old, and Jackson seemed to be just what we needed. I was intrigued by his caring and nurturing demeanor. He worked in a group home for developmentally disabled adults, whom I had the privilege of meeting during one of our first dates at a skating party for the residents of that home. I was moved by how much they adored Jackson. He also volunteered once a week, visiting an elderly woman to lift her spirits and keep her company. He was extremely helpful with my son, stepping into my life at a time when I had neither a reliable car nor babysitter and was never really sure how I would make it to class. Without hesitation, Jackson handed over the keys to his prized sports car and offered to watch my son so that I would not have to drop my courses for the semester. When he introduced me to three generations of women he deeply respected—his grandmother, mother, and younger sister—only two months after we met, that sealed the deal for me. Never before had I seen a man so affectionate and loving with the women in his family. My conclusion was clear: *Wow. That's how I'll be treated if I become one of them!* From that moment on, I was on a mission to make this man my husband.

But there was a different side of Jackson that everyone had warned me about. He loved women. I mean, *really* loved women, and everyone in our little college town knew it. He was a flirt and loved the attention he earned for his charm. Our relationship became a makeup-breakup cycle that began with my discovery of some girl he had been secretly messing around with and always ended with him crying and pleading for another chance. This time, he was a changed man, he'd say. And this time, he was much closer to becoming that man he'd always wanted to be, if only I'd give him a little more time. It was a deal.

After six years of this, we got married. No resolution. No improvement. Just marriage. I figured the situation would eventually resolve itself. It never occurred to me until much later that we were not actually in love. We married each other with hopes that this union would fill a void we each had in our lives. He aspired to do everything in his power to become a better man than his philandering father had been, and I wanted to complete the family unit I had started by providing a father for my son. So we forged ahead, pretending (and possibly even believing) that this could actually work. It didn't. Jackson had his strong points and made some progress over the years, but through the course of our marriage, he never became that man he had always told me he wanted to be. He struggled to shake the playboy mentality that he so proudly paraded during his college years. He never extended the love and affection to me that he had always given so freely to the women in his family, or even to the residents of that group home he worked with years before. And in spite of how helpful and involved Jackson was with my son when we first met, the two of them never really connected.

After five years of marriage, the birth of our beautiful daughter, and many disappointments, I found myself so desperate to escape that it hurt to stay. Literally. Just after my daughter was born, my instincts of his indiscretions were strong. I had no proof of what I thought he might be doing, but I *knew* what I knew. It was then that it became clear to me that I had two choices—to stay with him and accept that this is what my life was going to be, or to leave him and start over. My first decision was to stay and continue to do everything in my power to change him—counseling, prayer, patience, loyalty. I stuck around for two more years. After all, I had no proof. Only my instinct. I couldn't possibly end a marriage because I had an instinct, right? But my instinct was so strong that instead of praying for him to change, as I had done for nearly a decade, I began to pray desperately for clarity and truth.

And clarity and truth came—in a much more intense and eye-opening way than I could have ever prepared myself for. At the end of a very hot and depressing summer, when our daughter was just two years old, everything flew out into the open. Jackson managed to break the camel's back with yet another betrayal of my trust—a pattern of deception that began before I became pregnant and had continued on for three years. There was no rationalizing this one away. It was precisely what I had instinctively known all along. My heart grew cold, and I was done. That was it for me. I finally accepted that I was not going to change this man. I realized that the only person who could change him was *him* and that my staying provided no incentive for change. The counseling didn't work. My hanging in there with love, loyalty, and support didn't work. His apologies and dramatic expressions of remorse didn't work. After all that had been done to salvage this relationship, I packed up what little was left of me, and I walked away. *Perhaps his next wife will benefit from my strength.*

Once again, I had a lot of work to do. By that time, I had just earned my Ph.D. As great as that accomplishment was, I felt like an empty shell of a person on the inside. My self-esteem was shot. I had lost touch with my creative side, and I had totally numbed my heart and emotions. There was no life in me. I had been just going through the motions for so long, *the motions* had become who I was. This time around, I had even more to let go of and even more to rebuild than before.

Najee

My third relationship was not necessarily a relationship in the traditional sense, but it was the warmest, most unforgettable year of my life. Though short-lived, this was undoubtedly the most heartbreaking of the three because I had fallen in love for the first time and was totally caught off guard by it. I knew Najee for many years as an acquaintance before we became friends. The first time I met Najee, I had just broken off an engagement with Jackson after learning about yet another secret girlfriend of his only months after he proposed to me and only weeks after I moved across the country to begin our lives together. "I was going to break up with her before you moved here," he reasoned. Sure that I was done for good, I packed my things and moved to the other side of town. *That'll show him.*

I met Najee a few months later through a Christmas play we were both involved with. There was nothing spectacular about this meeting other than the fact that I felt a level of comfort in his presence that I had never experienced before. I distinctly remember being surprised by this strange sense of peace that came over me. We didn't speak much, but there was a definite attraction. Yet, whatever the feeling, I quickly dismissed it. At that point in my life, I was emotionally unavailable. My loyalty still belonged to Jackson. Though we were momentarily broken up, he was still the center of my world. Jackson was the only man I was able to see, so when he surprised me with my engagement ring and an apology at the stroke of midnight on New Year's Eve, I did what any senseless, hopeless romantic would do. I married him, of course.

It wasn't until two years later that I saw Najee again. This time, I was seven months pregnant and busy coordinating a poetry event. Just as before, our interactions were brief and professional. Unbeknownst to me, he was intrigued by me, but had such a respect for the institution of marriage that he dared not cross that line. I was so focused on my family, my career, and going to school that I didn't notice him until much later. Our professions—I, a campus event planner, and he, a performer—kept us in similar circles, so we remained acquaintances, exchanging polite hellos and head nods when our paths crossed.

But seven years after Najee and I first met, everything changed. The summer I left Jackson is when I *saw* Najee for the very first time. He was the first man my eyes opened up to see. And wow...what a sight he was! This man was handsome and intelligent and creative and sensitive. We became friends instantly, and the chemistry was unbelievable. I had no idea that it was possible to connect with a man in this way. It was perfection!

Najee was the one who encouraged my return to writing— the one who inspired poetry about love, peace, and happiness, even while I was in the trenches of a divorce. It was through him that I was able to find an oasis of love and support in the midst of what could have been a devastating series of events. We became each other's closest friend, and were wildly attracted to one another, but he made it a point early on to set boundaries to prevent tainting our friendship with physical and emotional drama. Of course, this only made me want him more.

Najee and I spent a great deal of time together. For a year, we'd lose track of time, spending entire afternoons chatting over slowly-eaten meals at mom and pop cafes. We'd spend hours on the phone as if we were teenagers in high school, talking about everything from politics to relationships, to our greatest dreams in life. He randomly uttered phrases like, "You are so amazing," and, "You're beautiful in every sense of the word," while staring at me with his gorgeous almond eyes. I had never heard a man speak those words to me before. He was wise and thoughtful and offered comfort and companionship like I had never experienced. No one had ever listened to me or cared about my thoughts and feelings the way that Najee had. He respected and admired me in ways that left me speechless.

Yet, as great as all of this was, we were not on the same page. My love for Najee managed to break through all of those well-intentioned boundaries that he set up in the beginning. Yes, I fell in *love*. Through those conversations, over many plates of waffles and omelets and cups of chai tea, and after all of those moments of uncontrolled laughter, I fell in love. He was intrigued and he cared deeply for me, but he resisted falling in love. I wanted to give him everything I had. He thought it was wiser to play it safe. He often reminded me that I had just ended a very long relationship and that he was facing some personal battles of his own. *Timing is everything,* he would say. I grew to loathe those words. It was because of this philosophy that he remained very adamant about not taking our friendship to the next level. I was devastated, pissed off, and confused, yet I had nothing but respect for his integrity.

But all of the respect in the world could not deny what I was feeling for this man. The fact that we were not on the same page put a strain on our friendship. Even after I relocated from the Midwest to Atlanta to take a job I couldn't refuse, we tried to carry it on because we cared deeply for one another. We tried, but as our enormous amounts of time together drastically came to a halt, and as I remained in love and in hope, it only became increasingly painful each time I was reminded that Najee was not in love with me. He didn't believe in long-distance relationships, so yet another barrier kept us from advancing our friendship. It finally occurred to me that I had to let go of this man who had done nothing but love and respect me, and who made me feel like the most beautiful woman in the world. I couldn't be with him. To say that it hurt like hell is an understatement. It felt like he took the breath out of me, and I was sure that only he could bring it back.

At that point, I had two choices—to obsess over what I couldn't have or to move forward with my life. I very reluctantly chose to move forward. We remained friends, but the friendship was just not the same. Living in different states, we could no longer meet up to eat and talk regularly, and we only touched bases over the phone a few times a month to check in on each other.

The emptiness was so loud, it was almost unbearable. Letting Najee go was more difficult than what I had experienced in my previous two relationships with Brian and Jackson. I missed him every moment of every day. I wanted more than anything to have my friend back. He was that good thing I had always dreamed of having in my life, and then he was gone. We didn't end on bitter terms. He remained one of my closest friends, but this made letting go even more difficult. I kept holding on to hope that one day he'd call to say that he had changed his mind and was moving to Atlanta. After a few tear-stained, straight-forward, painful conversations, I realized that I also had to let go of that *hope* so that letting him go and moving on with my life could be genuine and complete.

As different as each relationship was, I had some letting go to do after each was over. I laid out a strategy to move on and stuck to the plan. In these letters to you, I'll share some of these strategies with hopes that they may be helpful to you. As you read and begin to refocus, rebuild, and relove, take these ideas to heart. You'll notice that these strategies are flexible and can be adapted to address your specific situation. You may not need all of the strategies all of the time. Just take what you need and apply, apply, apply. What's most important is that you find a way to heal your heart and move forward to live an awesome and fulfilling life.

Love you,

Dr. Pamela

Letter 2

CHECK YOUR MOTIVES

If you love someone, let them go
If they return to you, they're yours to keep
If they don't return, it was never meant to be.

My Sister,

Remember that old saying about letting someone go and waiting to see if they return to you? I just heard it the other day, and it reminded me of something that I should address before we go any further. If you are letting them go with hopes that they will eventually come back to you as a fully evolved person, that they'll want you back once they've seen how much *you've* changed, or that they'll be sorry that you left them all alone, you are not letting him go. You are playing a game with them and with yourself—a game that can leave you even more hurt, torn, and disappointed than you are today. If you are serious about letting go, do it! Assume wholeheartedly that your life, never again, will be consumed with the life that you once had.

I'm not asking you to hate your ex. I'm asking you not to set yourself up. Because let's just say your plan works and they do come back. Does that mean that it is suddenly meant to be? Of course not. That quote can be very misleading. I mean, really...what are the odds that this is true for most people who are on the makeup/breakup cycle? How many times have you seen a couple that has no business being together make up and break up and make up again until *everyone's* heads are spinning? How many people welcomed back the wrong person, just because that person returned to them? Someone's return, in and of itself, does not make the relationship meant to be.

I'm definitely guilty of getting caught up in that fairytale way of thinking. I used to cultivate a vicious cycle of mind games with myself. *If I leave, he'll see that he'll never find another woman like me. He'll realize how great I really was.* Then I would leave a trail of breadcrumbs on my way out so that he'd know how to find his way back to my heart—and my exes always knew exactly what to say and do to get me back. I would assume that because he returned to me, flowers in hand with dampened eyes, it must mean that it was meant to be. Being on the opposite end of that storybook, I can tell you now that it *wasn't* meant to be. That old saying can trip you up. The story I told myself for years was that this was how my happily ever after would happen – via a broken, unhealthy or abusive relationship that would somehow repair itself instead of through the blossoming of a relationship that remained healthy and fulfilling from the start.

Remember this: if you're letting go for real, and you know that this is not a healthy situation for you, your reasons for leaving should be totally selfish and personal. This has to be about *you*. Perhaps you don't like the person you've become in their presence and you need *you* back. Maybe you're not finding fulfillment in this relationship, or you would prefer someone who adores you without having to beg and plead for the adoration. *Do you ever just think of me? I don't know who I am to you...* Whatever the reason, make sure that your departure is about making a better life for yourself. Letting go means that they are no longer a part of your decision-making process. You are the artist in chief.

If your reasons for letting go are all about the other person—they are always out too late, they yell at you, they cheat on you, they are not affectionate—then you can more easily be deceived into believing that if *they* change one of their flaws, this relationship can magically become the one that was meant to be. Don't do that to yourself. Change the trajectory of your own love story. Focus on *you* and redefine your reasons for letting go in a way that addresses improving the quality of *your* life. Not theirs.

Throughout the process of letting go of my failed marriage, I acknowledged that Jackson was a good person, but simply not the best person for me. Yes, he did some things that many would agree warranted my decision to leave. I eventually learned, however, to make leaving about what I needed to do for me, and not about what he did or didn't do for me. I did not like the person I had become around him. I was insecure, had low expectations for respect, and was desperately unhappy. We were not a good fit for each other.

As soon as I stopped making my unhappiness about Jackson's unwillingness to stay faithful, I realized that it didn't matter whether or not he came back with promises. It didn't matter how well he would do *this* time around. I was not the best person I could be with him in my life. I had lost sight of the creative, lively soul I had always been before he and I got together. It wasn't until I realized that my need to let go was not about making a point to Jackson, but about preserving *me*, that I was able to really begin letting go. I was on a mission to preserve me by any means necessary—by changing my phone number, leaving the state, keeping busy, doing whatever I needed to do to break those emotional ties.

As you are letting go, be willing to do so with full acceptance of the worst-case scenario. Accept that they will never come back, will never change, that this chapter of your life is forever *over*. If you expect or hope for anything more than that, you are not really letting go. You may, in fact, find that what you *think* might be a worst-case scenario is actually the best-case scenario ever! That said, you should understand that leaving to make a point or to give each other space to make changes has its place and can even be a successful move in some cases. My assumption, however, is that you have come to a place where you know in your heart that you need to let go completely and move on to a new place in life. So, as long as you're still leaving breadcrumbs, you are not truly letting go.

Since we don't live fairytale lives and because sometimes when something is over, it is really actually over, let's rewrite our nifty little inspirational quote so that it more accurately reflects reality. I've got two versions for you to play with:

If you love someone (*who is not meant for you*),
let them go.
If they return to you, let them go.
If they don't return, let them go.

If you love someone (*who is not worthy of you*),
let them go.
If they return to you, don't open the door,
If they don't return, praise God that you're free,
and then let go!

You are the artist! Use the lines below to recreate this quote and make it your own. Replace the parenthetic phrases with whatever words best fit your situation. It doesn't matter how you word it or how much you change it. Do whatever works for you, so long as you get the point.

Love you!

Dr. Pamela

♥ **INSPIRE YOUR HEART**

_____

_____

_____

_____

_____

Letter 3

LET THE JOURNEY BEGIN

My Sister,

After Najee, I spent many days just exhausted from tears and flat-out confused about what went wrong. I found myself consumed with regret for all of the decisions—good and bad—that I made with him along the way. At the moment, it seemed that he was the only one made for me, that no other man could possibly take his place. Have you had moments like this? These moments and this flurry of emotions are the worst. They can make you feel like you're crazy. The very thought of letting go is agonizing, especially when you're trying to let go of someone you were deeply connected with, someone you invested so much time in, someone you have given a great deal of yourself to.

But know this: you were created to live a fulfilling life, complete with love and companionship. You have much to accomplish with your life—much to live for, much yet to experience. Don't sell yourself short. If you follow the right path and focus on strengthening yourself over the next year, you'll experience a new level of living. You'll be a better person. You'll find better love. You'll enjoy a better life. But this cannot happen until you let go.

I know it's scary and that it's not necessarily what you *want* to do. That's okay. This process was never meant to be easy. These challenges—this peeling away of your layers, the nakedness, the exposure—can be painful and embarrassing. It all may seem to be outrageously unbearable. It really sucks to be at this place in life. And it sucks even more because it seems like you have absolutely no control over the situation. The relationship is done. What you believed to be the love of your life is out of your reach, and no matter how hard you try to make it right, things only seem to get worse.

But I'm going to let you in on something. You do have control. Lots of it. You have complete and total control over your own life and what you do with it from this point forward. In fact, you have *more* control than you had when you were involved with your ex, because now your decisions involve one less person. This gives you more freedom and space than before to focus on your needs and to get those needs met. You are the artist.

But let's not sugar coat this experience. What you're feeling right now may not go away overnight. Whenever anything breaks, it takes time for it to be repaired or repurposed before it can fully heal. Be fair and allow yourself the time you need. Be diligent in doing whatever is necessary to get healed and clear about what you want so that you don't find yourself back on their doorstep with a ticket to one more ride on the emotional rollercoaster that used to be your relationship.

If you hang in there, you can rise up as a wiser, stronger, and more loving person as you overcome this obstacle. I challenge you to focus on improving yourself so that this time next year, you can reflect back on this experience with great pride and reverence for how far you've come. It's definitely possible. As a matter of fact, it is *more* than possible if you are serious about moving forward with your life.

Everything I share with you is my own unchangeable truth—
pieces of my own story and lessons from my own life that I've
managed to piece together as the artist of my own life. Having a
plan helped me move forward each time I had my heart broken.
Through this process, I discovered that I am truly a beautiful
person who is fully deserving of every bit of peace, joy, and
happiness that I desire. I took the time to discover this truth for
myself, to believe it, and to remind myself of it daily. Knowing
that this was possible allowed me to step away from the
disappointments and failures of my past and move into the
direction of a life I wanted to live. I want the same for you!

So step away—slowly if you have to, but step away—and
avoid looking back. Moving forward and upward is not easy, but
you can do it. I found that what was ahead of me was much
greater than what I left behind. This can be your own truth, your
own story. Letting go can give you a clear and strong mind—a
mind that allows you to better discern who should and should
not be in your life, and what you should or should not sacrifice.
If you're vulnerable, you're more likely to let just anyone in for
the sake of having someone there. That is a very dangerous door
to open just after experiencing heartbreak. So, in order to get
you back on track and to ensure that you're headed in the right
direction, we'll work on bringing the broken pieces together by
learning how to refocus, rebuild, and relove. Beginning with my
next letter, I'll guide you through the process of refocusing.

Love you,

Dr. Pamela

THE ART OF
REFOCUSING

CHAPTER TWO

REFOCUS WITH OTHER PEOPLE

Those who really love you will speak the truth to you at the risk of falling out with you. Loving truth from a friend is better than gold.

– T.D. Jakes Ministries
Facebook Post, January 3, 2013

Letter 4

GET YOUR MIND RIGHT

My Sister,

Shortly after I left Jackson, I found myself in a whirlwind of emotions. I was consumed with anger and overcome with sadness at the same time At any given moment, I would go from cursing him under my breath to sobbing uncontrollable tears without warning. Have you experienced days like this? If you have, please know that this is normal. You're dealing with a loss, and that's not easy. I remember how I kept playing out all of the what-ifs and the regrets in my head. *What if I had done this differently? Oh, I so regret giving him that! How could I be so stupid? How could he be so insensitive? What a jerk after all that I gave him...*

Maybe in your case, your ex wasn't a jerk at all. Maybe it was *you* who messed up and you're dealing with the regret of that. Either way, my sister, it's important that you reduce the amount of energy you spend thinking about them, the scenario, and what went wrong. It is time to refocus. I know it's not easy. It won't happen naturally. This is why it takes strategy to heal after a broken heart. So, let's take a look at our first strategy: *refocusing.*

When you refocus, you choose to commit your time, attention, and energy to new central points of interest. There are a few benefits to refocusing. First, the amount of energy you spend thinking about your ex will begin to diminish. Second, focusing on other aspects of your life gives you an outlet—a place to turn when you feel yourself dwelling on what you no longer have. And third, refocusing gives you the opportunity to work on improving your own life. When you choose to stay focused on those things that you *can* change and improve, you are taking the first steps necessary to get him out of the forefront of your mind and move on. When your mind is consumed with your ex, the relationship, and all that went wrong, it is nearly impossible to move on. Start with refocusing. I'm going to address three different aspects of your life to focus on: other people, your priorities, and your goals. Let's talk about other people first.

Other People

How are you doing in the friendship department? Who are the people around you? Who loves you? I hope that you have not isolated yourself. I hope that you are surrounded with a good group of people who love you and have your back. Now is the time to develop new friendships and nurture those old ones. Often times, *other people* are the most effective agents of refocusing after experiencing a loss of any sort. Other people can help us laugh, reflect, cry, rejoice, and even temporarily forget. Other people can keep us in check when we are tempted to slide backwards and need a dose of reality. Other people can build us up when we are feeling down or when we begin to second-guess ourselves. Other people can be an integral part of letting go.

But there is a flip side. Other people can also be damaging and can cause you to regress rather than move forward. This is why it's important to be intentionally selective about who you let surround and influence you when times are difficult. Don't let just anyone who will listen into your circle. Below is a simple overview of some personality and motive types broken down into three categories. In the next few letters, I'll tell you about people to avoid, people to approach with caution, and people to embrace. You know them. They're at your job, in your family, and among your friends. It's important that you recognize who they are. In my next letter, we'll start with people to avoid.

Love,

Dr. Pamela

AVOID	APPROACH WITH CAUTION	EMBRACE
The Pooper Scooper	The Mutual Friend	The Uplifter
The Self-Righteous Judge	The Colleague	The Life Processor
The Hopeless Romantic	The Social Networking Friend	The Voice of Experience
The Baggage Carrier		

Letter 5

PEOPLE TO AVOID

My Sister,

When I was going through my divorce, I noticed that most people were more than willing to lend a listening ear because they wanted to know what was going on. They wanted the *scoop*. I had to be wise about what I told to whom. I had to be conscious of who was there to listen and offer support, versus those who were there to listen for entertainment purposes only. It was clear that there were certain types of people to whom I could gravitate and those whom I needed to avoid. In this letter we'll look at the pooper scoopers, self-righteous judges, hopeless romantics, and baggage carriers. Be on the lookout!

The Pooper Scooper

The name says it all. The Pooper Scooper are the folks who are hungry for your crappy stories—your failures, phobias, and flings. They want to know the scoop and all the juicy details. These people are *great* listeners and may have even mastered the art of responding with compassion. There are two types of scoopers—the gossipers and the predators. You'll recognize the gossipers because they are the same ones who come to you to get the scoop on someone else, or the ones who will tell you the latest thing they've heard. Steer clear of these folks unless you *want* your business out there. Just rest assured that when your story is retold, it will be fabricated with new twists and extra drama—just for effect.

Gossiping scoopers come up from behind, scoop up your crap, take it home, spice it up, and spread it around the neighborhood, the workplace, the family, the internet— wherever they have access. They've always hated and envied you. They *live* for the opportunity to bask in the glory of your crap, especially if they are one of those people who have been waiting and aching to see you fail at something. Yes, your crap makes them feel elevated.

Predatory scoopers are ingeniously slick with the game. Like gossipers, predators are great listeners and are hungry to get the scoop on your life, but this is not for the sheer joy of getting the gossip. No. A predator's goal is to find your weakness and figure out how to use it to their advantage. They love to play hero to the damsel in distress. Perhaps your predator is attracted to you and sees your despair as a prime opportunity to take advantage of your vulnerability. Or maybe they are a colleague searching for an angle that will allow them to finally outdo you. These predatory scoopers resemble gossipers in that their eyes sparkle at the sight of your crap. They'll gladly scoop it up with hopes that they can somehow benefit from the chaos in your life. Predators are even more dangerous because their goal is to climb their way to success on your head while leading you to believe that they want to help you. Don't be deceived. Both can bring you harm. Be very careful about who you share your business with. Look around. Who are the scoopers in your life? Take down their names. And stay out of dodge!

The Self-Righteous Judge

We all have overly opinionated people in our lives—people who are so opinionated that all other points of view are sinful, ignorant, or just flat-out wrong. If you don't think the way they think, they'll harp on it until you actually begin to question yourself for having a different point of view. Besides the obvious, the problem with these people is that if your current situation does not jibe with their beliefs, they can really tear down your self-esteem and leave you questioning whether or not you're doing the right thing.

When I was going through my divorce, I confided in an old friend. This was a friend who years before had sat me down to explain that Jackson wasn't right for me. So when I left him, I was sure that this friend would fully support me and understand my predicament. To my surprise, her response was quite the opposite. She essentially told me that it didn't matter how miserable I was, or that he had repeatedly betrayed my trust, or that I finally felt free and back on track after leaving. None of that mattered. She informed me that because I had disobeyed God many years ago and married Jackson anyway, that I needed to stay and continue to suffer the consequences. If I waited it out, remained submissive, and prayed for him, eventually, I would be rewarded. Eventually.

In horror, I pictured myself sixty-five years old, and Jackson, nearly seventy, finally opening his eyes to the beautiful, yet aged, quiet woman who had always been there for him. What a shame that this beautiful woman, ill from quietly enduring all of the years of neglect, infidelity, and stress only had weeks to live. But, at least he eventually came around.

This was not the life that I was born to live. And perhaps, it wouldn't have been quite *that* horrible. But really, who's to say that it wouldn't have been? What I did know was that I had made a huge mistake by ignoring the warnings of concerned family and friends and the signs that presented themselves each step of the way—right up through our wedding day. I knew immediately that I had made a mistake. This is not to say that all shaky relationships, questionable situations, and terrible mistakes should be painted with the same brush. Some can and should be worked out. But some require us to flee. And flee, I did.

Leaving Jackson was not one of my hard-headed moments of rebellion. This was my response to what was undoubtedly God's grace and mercy. I was given another chance at life. I disagreed with the view that God was glaring down upon me with lips pressed together, whip in hand, ready to strike if I chose to backtrack and undo the mistake I had made. I couldn't accept that I would be expected to stay in a situation that was never right for me in the first place as a punishment for not making the right decision years ago.

What I needed around me during this difficult time in my life was love, not judgment. I drew the line at flat-out disrespect, self-righteousness, and disregard for my well-being. The self-righteous judges in my life (there were a few of them) crossed that line. My decision to let Jackson go was non-negotiable. I wasn't looking for advice about what to do. I needed support. So, I turned away from those who were judgmental and focused on my sources of support.

The Hopeless Romantic

Hopeless romantics mean no harm. I have been one myself. A hopeless romantic becomes a problem when romance—not logic—becomes all that matters. When you are in the process of letting go, the last thing you need is someone in your ear painting an overly romanticized picture of you and your ex reconciling and living happily ever after, especially when you know in your heart that it's over and that it *should* be over. These romantic fantasies are counter-productive. If you allow yourself to go there, you are not letting go.

Your hopeless romantic usually has the best of intentions. Perhaps it's a friend of yours who had no idea that things were bad between you and your ex. She may have been intrigued by how "cute" the two of you were together, and because we get so caught up in how cute a couple is, this typically works like a charm. She, along with all of your other close connections and social media friends may have been living vicariously through you, believing that if you could have this perfect, awesome relationship, then she could too. If your fairytale fantasy doesn't work, then *her* whole world is shattered. Not just yours. Hers. She doesn't mean to be this selfish. She just wants it to work out. She's wearing rose-colored lenses and is caught up with what will make *her* feel better – the survival of *your* relationship.

"But you guys were just soooo cute together!" Never mind that this toxic relationship involves emotional neglect, physical abuse, or a partner who doesn't believe in your dreams.

Your hopeless romantic knows this. But she pretends that that it isn't as bad as it seems (this, by the way, is an example of gaslighting). All that matters to her is that you are your ex are just so cute together, and your breakup is shattering her dreams. Don't shatter her dreams. Give her some space until *she* has found a way to let go. Don't let her drag you into her fantasy world. If you know in your heart that it is supposed to be over, don't entertain these types of conversations. Talk to her about other stuff, or don't talk to her at all. Do what you have to do to take care of *you*.

Baggage Carrier

Like the hopeless romantic, the baggage carrier is a bit delusional. This person also paints a skewed picture of reality. Except, instead of giving you a false sense of hope, the baggage carrier offers a real sense of despair. This is worse because it can cause you to become embittered and angry, which is sure to keep all potential joy and success far, far away from you. When going through a breakup and trying to let go, we are already tempted enough to sink into a place of gloom and doom. We don't need someone to add to that for us by convincing us that all men suck, that women are overly emotional, that everyone cheats, that marriage is a farce, or that love does not really exist. People who think this way have some letting go of their own to do. They are definitely not in a position to guide you through this process.

For the record, let me say that love does exist and love can happen for you. You attract to yourself what you put out. If you live your life with bitterness, everything you do will be inspired by that bitterness. Everything will be clouded with fear and doubt. If you live an empowered and love-filled life, everything you do will be inspired by love, empowerment, and confidence. This is how you attract the same to yourself. Don't get caught up and dragged down by others who live and believe hopelessly. You are at a point in your life where you are working on going in the opposite direction. Where they are is not where you aspire to be.

Let's recap. The people you do not want to talk to about your situation are the pooper scoopers, the self-righteous judges, the hopeless romantics, and the baggage carriers. They have nothing good to offer you at this time. I'm not suggesting that you shut these people out of your life, because that simply may not be reasonable or possible in all cases (like, for example, if one of those people happen to be your mother). I am suggesting that you remain fully aware, intentional, and wise about what you do discuss with them or in their presence. Don't allow yourself to get sucked into any of their unhealthy, unproductive, and debilitating ways of thinking and living. You can live above that.

I'm going to let you chew on that for a minute and take some time to think about who these people may be in your life. How will you interact with them? How will you ensure that you do not get sucked in? This is an important strategy for staying focused and on track. In my next letter, I'll tell you about three types of people to approach with caution, not because of how they think or act, per se, but because of how you are associated with them.

Until then, make a list of your pooper scoopers, your self-righteous judges, your hopeless romantics, and your baggage carriers. You may not be able to identify all of them now, but if anyone you know has these qualities, they will reveal themselves along the way. Be careful and stay aware.

Love you,

Dr. Pamela

❤ **INSPIRE YOUR HEART**

Take a second to think about the people in your life who need to be avoided at this time:

People to Avoid
Pooper Scoopers:
Self-Righteous Judges:
Hopeless Romantics:
Baggage Carriers:

Letter 6

PEOPLE TO APPROACH WITH CAUTION

My Sister,

As you refocus by paying attention to the other people in your life, it's important to be aware of who are talking to. Everyone is not equal and should not know everything. In my previous letter, I wrote of the folks who should be avoided. Now, I want to tell you about those who should be approached with caution. These are people who are risky to talk to, primarily because of how you are associated with them. There are three categories of people I encountered that I would recommend handling with caution: the mutual friend, the colleague, and the social media friend.

The Mutual Friend

Three years into my on-again-off-again relationship with Jackson, he left California and transferred to a different university. So, when we got engaged, it was I who sold my house, packed up my son and moved from California to the foreign lands of the Midwest. By this time, Jackson had been there for two years and had a generous set of friends. Some of those friends, over time, became my friends. This issue of the mutual friend was especially challenging for me when we broke up. Because I relocated, almost *everyone* I knew were our mutual friends, so my support network nearly disappeared after our divorce, while his remained well intact. The reality was, they were really his friends first. They had been gracious enough to welcome me into their circles only because I was Jackson's wife.

When our marriage ended, suddenly all of these people (some of whom I had come to genuinely admire) were people I didn't know whether or not I should trust. Some were abundantly clear about where their loyalties lay and immediately dropped me from their friend lists (literally *and* figuratively). I honestly can't fault them for that. It was shocking at first because losing my connection with our mutual friends was not something that I had considered or prepared for. I mean surely, since I had always been a great wife, mother, and friend, everyone would still have my back. *Right?*

No. Not right at all. But, really, what did I expect? They didn't become his friends because of his ability or inability to be a great boyfriend or husband. That part of his life was irrelevant to them. They were connected to him before he became a husband or father, so the context of those friendships was bigger and more historical than what happened between him and me.

There were a few mutual friends who managed to gracefully stay out of the middle and maintain friendships with each of us independently. In such cases, especially when I was knee-deep in my efforts to move on, I was very cautious about how I interacted with them. I never initiated contact, and I was careful about what I communicated if they contacted me. When I did speak with the mutual friends, it was purely under the assumption that anything I said would be communicated back to Jackson. If there was something I didn't want him to know, I kept it to myself. On the other hand, if there was something I didn't mind him knowing, or something I actually *wanted* him to know, I'd share it.

Why bother engaging in this dance with mutual friends at all? I am not into game-playing, so my decision to dance around what I should and should not say was primarily to remain cordial. I kept contact to an absolute minimum. The choice to interact with the mutual friends is yours to make, based on the circumstances of your own situation. I didn't have much contact with the mutual friends after the breakup—perhaps one or two conversations, tops. The fewer interactions you have with your mutual friends, the easier it is for you to let go of that chapter of your life and move on.

I know it's not always that easy. Especially if, for example, you and your ex's sister had become really close. Again, I'm not suggesting that you cut ties and set bridges on fire. Just be careful about what you say and how much you share about your life. As time goes on and as you become less attached, maintaining friendships with the mutual friends may be easier and less risky. For one thing, you will have had more time and a clearer mind for determining who is truly in your corner. Second, you don't risk jeopardizing your ability to move on by getting sucked back into your old circles, old habits, old relationships, and old mistakes. Give yourself time and space to start anew and to redefine who you are *without* him.

The Colleague

Take caution when spilling your business to colleagues. Everyone's work situation is different. Some people work in very hostile and rigid environments, while others consider their colleagues and co-workers to be like family. Regardless of your situation, I highly recommend that you proceed with caution. Even if you are sure that everyone at work has your back, you can never really be sure that *everyone* at work has your back. Don't let your life become the reality drama series of the workplace. Even well-intentioned people fail to understand the value of respecting someone else's privacy by keeping information to themselves.

I'm not suggesting that you keep the fact that your relationship ended a secret, especially if it is one that everyone knows about. Sometimes it is actually easier (and healthier) to just say it than to plaster a smile on your face and pretend that all is well. However, your colleagues certainly do not need to know all of the juicy details of your life. It's difficult to know if or how you'll be judged by colleagues, especially those who have strong opinions about how relationships should be handled. Will they start judging your work performance? Could airing your dirty laundry result in less respect and fewer opportunities? Or will explaining your life circumstances allow others to give you the time, space, and understanding needed to heal and move forward? It really depends on your work environment and your level of comfort with sharing.

I was fortunate because I had just transitioned out of a toxic work environment and into one that resembled a caring family. As colleagues, we supported one another through personal ups and downs, such as the birth of children, death of parents, financial struggles, and in my case, a divorce. Our team was one that openly discussed these personal challenges, so I felt safe enough to share what was going on in my life.

It was only a matter of time before my colleagues noticed that something was wrong. My poker face has never been very good. I was often in a daze at work—totally unfocused at my desk and discretely enraged during department meetings. I was unproductive, unfocused, and detached from colleagues. This was highly uncharacteristic of me. If I didn't say or do something, I was going to explode, so I chose to tell my boss in the most spontaneous way ever. I slipped him a note during a faculty meeting.

As my colleagues were actively engaging in discussions about course offerings, partnerships, and student issues, I was sitting there having a moment—fuming, fighting back tears, and suppressing the urge to completely lose it. *I gave my all to that man!* I was ready to start turning tables over. So instead of creating an unforgettable scene during this meeting, I pulled out a piece of paper and let my pen speak the truth. I politely slipped the note to our department chair and excused myself from the room. My words were simple, but effective:

> *I'm sorry, but I am having a very difficult week. I just found out that Jackson was unfaithful and I left him two days ago. If I don't leave this meeting now, I will have a meltdown in front of everyone. Thanks for understanding. –Pamela*

After he read my note, he also left the meeting and caught me in the hallway to offer his support. I was in an amazingly supportive environment. My supervisor was incredibly understanding and accommodating, as I knew he would be. He and my colleagues encouraged me to do what I needed to do to be okay. And I did just that. I took the week off and spent some time with family. I was so blessed to have that type of support.

The problem, however, is that because I *did* do what I needed to do to be okay (maybe a little too much of it), everyone knew that Pamela was going through a divorce. I felt like the damsel in distress who needed help and support, and was no longer the strong, resilient woman who could be awesome at all that she does, no matter what was going on in her personal life. It placed a magnifying glass on what I wasn't doing well. Even if my colleagues chalked it up to the fact that I was going through a lot, I still believed that they perceived me as being less adequate. This proved to be a bit of a setback for me, because I became insecure in my work and overly concerned about what they thought of me.

I will say that because I happened to be in a transitional period in my career and because I was given the flexibility and support to do what I needed to do to get myself in order, I don't regret opening my mouth. Had this happened in a permanent or more critical phase in my career, I certainly would have handled it differently. I would have found more creative ways to get the flexibility and support I needed so that I was not overwhelmed by my work and to prevent my productivity and value from suffering.

Do what you have to do to make your work situation work for you, but be sure that if you choose to discuss your situation with supervisors and colleagues, that you do so with caution and that you have a plan.

The Social Media Friend

Assume that *nothing* you do online is totally private. Also assume that you're not always "talking" to the person you think you're talking to when chatting, emailing, posting, or blogging online. Proceed with caution.

I made a huge social media mistake shortly after I left Jackson. This surprises me because I am usually pretty technologically savvy. But somehow, while communicating with a friend (during the early days of Facebook), I accidentally posted on my public wall, "Yes, girl, it's over. I left Jackson. He was cheating." I didn't realize my mistake until an hour later when one of my good friends (who knows it's not like me to make such a public announcement) sent me a private message asking if I had intended for the statement to be visible to the public. *Shoot!*

I was horrified! I wasn't ready to bring the general public in on such a personal issue, and even if I had been, I certainly wouldn't have wanted any details, particularly the reason why we broke up, publicly announced. I didn't want to answer any questions, and I especially didn't want this to be picked up by my pooper scoopers.

I scrambled to undo what I had just done—well...what I had done AN HOUR AGO. As you can imagine, it was too late, because in cyber time an hour is like letting two days pass. Already, the story had been picked up by a scooper, who called a friend of mine to find out whether or not it was true. My friend, in turn, called to warn me that the story was making its rounds. *Perfect.*

I allowed this to happen because in that moment, I was careless. Looking back, I believe I was in a numb state of mind where I was just going through the motions. I was simply trying to get through the day. The month. The rest of the year. Please don't do what I carelessly did. Try not to go numb. Be aware and be deliberate with your actions. Stay on top of things and be careful.

The other issue I've had with social media is not knowing who's *really* on the other end of the computer screen. For a about a year, someone who had created various fake aliases repeatedly contacted me, asking to be included in my network of online "friends." I didn't know who this person was at first, but I had a feeling that she was connected to one of my exes. I knew that these attempts to connect with me were for the sole purpose of getting into my personal business by keeping tabs on what I was doing, who I was connected with, and what kind of mindset I was maintaining. Now, *this* is something that I wasn't quite so sloppy or careless about. I never accepted requests from people I didn't know personally, so each time one of these fake alias requests came through, they were very easy to detect.

I noticed that one of the fake aliases had successfully connected to some of my friends to appear legit, but when I asked my friends if they knew this person, they all said that they did not. When I began to ask the alias very pointed questions about her identity and her intentions, she stopped responding. When I sent her a message stating that I was documenting everything and intended to report her...*poof!* Like magic, the profile disappeared from the face of cyber earth. I eventually figured out who this person was, and in hindsight, I am *so* glad that I never accepted the request to connect.

Be careful. Be aware of whom you're talking to and what information you're putting out there. If you do post information on a public forum, be sure that you are strategic about it and that it is information you *want* people (assume all people) to have. A good piece of advice I once heard on a radio show (particularly for people going through a divorce—but great information for all) was to avoid posting or sending messages about the breakup, because any of it can prove to be incriminating should your ex choose to use it against you in a court of law. If there are kids involved, resist posting information or pictures about your wild party-girl episodes (that includes those aerobic pole-dancing classes). You never know when or if a custody battle can ensue, and if that happens, the last thing you want is for your character as a mom to be questioned and trashed by a lawyer, a judge, and twelve jurors. Watch your back, protect yourself, and be careful.

My last suggestion about social media is simple. Go through the list of people who are connected to you, those who have access to your profile, and be sure that they are people you still feel comfortable being connected with. If not...delete! Don't worry about hurting feelings or offending anyone. Your security and peace of mind are much more important than that.

Remember to proceed with caution when interacting with mutual friends, co-workers, and online social networking friends. That way you can minimize the extra drama that can creep up in your life. Haven't you already had enough? By staying away from certain folks who don't have your best interests at heart (pooper scoopers, dishonorable judges, hopeless romantics, and baggage carriers), and by keeping your business off of the web, you will be able to more easily move forward and continue to focus on the greatness that lies ahead of you. Refuse to allow yourself to be pulled backwards by these folks. Insist on taking care of you.

Take a look at the box on the next page and think about how you will handle interactions with your mutual friends, colleagues, and those social networking friends. Go ahead and take some time to jot down a few strategies. I hope this helps, Sis.

Love,

Dr. Pamela

♥ **INSPIRE YOUR HEART**

How I will handle interactions with:
Mutual Friends:
Colleagues:
Social Media Connections:

Letter 7

PEOPLE TO EMBRACE

My Sister,

There will be times when you'll need to breathe, when you'll want to let your guard down and be totally transparent. There will be times when you just want to be human and let it all out. It's fine to do this when you're alone, but it's even better to do this among people you love and trust, and who, of course, love and trust you.

After all three of my breakups, while I was in the midst of letting go, I was blessed to have found some people who stood in my corner to give me pointers, who nursed away the blood, sweat, and tears, and who encouraged me to keep fighting. They were my heart healers. They kept me going. Each healer had a specific purpose. When I say that it was a blessing to have *found* these people, I mean it exactly in that way, because I had to reach out and make it known that I needed the support. I had to swallow my pride and admit to myself that I could not do this in a healthy manner alone. I had to select wisely and be sure that these people were genuine, and that they truly had my best interests at heart. I also had to be willing to wholeheartedly accept the support that they offered.

It has always been easier for me to slap on a smile and keep moving forward than it has been to admit defeat and reach out for the help I need. After leaving Brian and Jackson, I knew in each case that what I was dealing with was no light transition. I needed support. I needed to talk to people I could trust, who wouldn't judge me, and who wanted to help me find happiness again. Having these people in my corner was a major factor in my ability to let go and move on the way that I did.

Find your entourage of heart healers. It doesn't have to be a large one (and it probably shouldn't be). All you need are three essentials: an uplifter, a life processor, and a voice of experience. If you're fortunate enough to have more than one of each, by all means, embrace them! If one person is so awesome that they can assume more than one of these roles, that's great! Are there people currently in your life who would fit really well into one of these roles? If not, go out and find them. One woman, who became my voice of experience, came from an unexpected connection. She was my pastor, and I had reached out to her for prayer. After meeting with her several times, I learned that she had experienced some of the heartbreak that I was feeling. When I found this out, I snatched her up and added her to my entourage.

But before I tell you anything more, let me first back up and explain what I mean by uplifter, life processor, and voice of experience, and why you should embrace them.

The Uplifter

An uplifter is a person who isn't afraid to tell you that you're awesome. Plain and simple. They help to boost your self-esteem when you're questioning your worth. They drag you out of the house for some good laughs when you're wallowing in self-pity. They point out all of the reasons why that ex never deserved you in the first place and will have your back if they so much as looks at you the wrong way (even if the breakup was *your* fault).

Uplifters are so important to have around because breaking up and letting go can be a lonely and depressing process. Even if you're doing all of the right things and you're making progress, it is still essential that you laugh from time to time, that you don't always cry alone, and that you are regularly reminded of how great you really are.

My uplifters were a critical part of my healing, particularly the uplifters I had after my divorce. I needed them because the vast majority of my acquaintances had been Jackson's friends or colleagues. After we separated, I felt nearly abandoned in the Midwest. My uplifters saved my life. I had three uplifters—two out of town and one in town. They each had their own special way of lifting me up, and even though they didn't all know each other, they collectively kept me going. On days when I just wanted to lay around and be pissed off, one of them was my "Oh, hell naw!" girl who would drag me out of the house for a walk, a drink, or a good meal. When I started questioning whether or not I was doing the right thing and how this all was affecting my two-year-old daughter, my uplifters reminded me that what I chose to stand up for sets an important example for her.

What's most interesting about my experience is that two of my uplifters were not the usual suspects. They weren't old friends, and they weren't people I had confided in before. I had to build that sort of bond with them by being willing to open up and by choosing wisely. I knew that I needed the support, so I made sure that I had it. It's so easy to allow your misery to be magnified by the belief that no one cares about what's going on in your life. I know. I allowed myself to go there on those rare occasions when all three of my uplifters couldn't be reached. Don't let yourself to sit in that mental space of despair. Somebody does care, and somebody will support you, but only if you're willing to reach out and let someone know that you need it.

The Life Processor

Najee proved to be an amazing life processor after my divorce. We frequently met up over meals and would sit for hours as I lamented over what had happened in my failed relationship and worried about would come of my future. He was one of those even-tempered types who patiently listened and then, like magic, would say something that made perfect sense. If I suddenly announced that I was going to do something totally irrational, he would ask question after question after question until I realized, *Oh my God, that would be a really stupid move, wouldn't it?*

In some ways, my uplifters did this too, but my life processors were different because their role was not primarily to make me feel good. It was to make me *think*—to help me process what I've learned from the experience and what I would do differently next time. In fact, sometimes the tough love and truths they revealed about myself didn't feel good at all, but they were all truths that I needed to hear. I needed to hear (from Najee) that I was just as responsible for the failure of my marriage as Jackson was. I knew that we weren't ready and that we had some serious pre-marital issues to address, but I made the decision to ignore those issues and forge ahead anyway. I needed to hear (from my mom) that I had expected too much, too quickly from Najee, and that I needed to take time to rebuild myself before trying to jump into another relationship. And I needed to hear (from my girlfriend, Carla) that the pattern in *all* of my relationships was the same: that had I lost sight of the fact that I have much to offer to another person, and that I should never have to beg or compromise my dignity to keep someone in my life.

My life processors challenged me to step it up and get ready for the next phase of my life. It's very important that your life processor is willing to be brutally honest and frank with you about what they see. Not cruelly, of course, but also not passively. They shouldn't have a tendency to dance around the truth. Because if the message is so sugar-coated that you miss the point, well, that definitely doesn't help you. And if you want your life processor to be truly effective, you've got to be open-minded enough to *hear* the truth. Being defensive doesn't help. You'll find that your best life processors will be able to break through those defensive barriers to get to the heart of the matter. Just don't make it more difficult than it needs to be. After all, it's *you* who stands to benefit from this more than anyone else, so swallow your pride and let your life processors get to work.

The Voice of Experience

The key word here is "experience." Your voice of experience has been where you are and is now where you want to be—free from the makeup-breakup cycle and at peace with the fact that the relationship has ended. They have long moved on. They can empathize with you and give you great insight on how to move forward. So, while the duty of your uplifters is to keep you from wallowing in self-pity, and the role of your life processors is to challenge you to look at yourself, your voice of experience's task is to inspire and empower you. *Inspire* you to believe that you can let go and pass on tools that will *empower* you to let go.

To be in contact with a living inspiration who has walked and breathed through what you are experiencing is priceless, particularly if that person has gained more strength and wisdom as a result. If that's where you want to be, get under the wing of someone who's been there. This person's story doesn't need to identically resemble yours. In fact, you may learn even more if their story has twists and turns that are different from the twists and turns in your own. If you have the opportunity to soak up the wisdom of someone who's openly willing to share, scoot in close, pick their brain, and take in the nuggets of wisdom from her experience.

Just be sure that your voice of experience meets two criteria: they have truly let go (with no evidence of bitterness, anger, or resentment), and they have your best interests at heart. Otherwise, you risk allowing this person to pull you back down the hill of progress and into the valley of misery. Make sure that your voice of experience is someone who will help you in your upward climb.

Fortunately, one of my voices of experience, Pastor Melva Henderson, also happened to be my spiritual mentor. Through her, I was able to reap the benefits of having both in one person. As a matter of fact, my entourage of heart healers (my uplifters, my life processors, and my voices of experience) consisted of a few people who overlapped and sometimes played double roles. My friend Carla, for example, alternated regularly between being an uplifter and a life processor. She'd get me out of the house for some fun, but then she would proceed to pick my brain about a number of topics from what my game plan was to how I would avoid finding myself in a similar situation in the future.

It's a great thing if you have people who play dual or multiple roles, but if not, that's okay. What's important is that all three roles are fulfilled and that you are refocusing. Be sure that you embrace people who will uplift you, help you process your journey, and who can inspire and empower you to let go. These are the people who will be integral to your growth and your ability to remain healthy and strong throughout this process. They'll provide support, insight, and most importantly, laughter. Reach out for it. Accept it. You deserve it. No one should have to go the road alone—and you, my friend, are no exception.

Much love,

Dr. Pamela

♥ INSPIRE YOUR HEART

My Heart Healers
Uplifters
Life Processors
Voices of Experience

How will I recruit people to fill any vacant positions? Who can I reach out to?

Letter 8

DON'T LOSE YOUR SPARK

My Sister,

Not too long ago, I had dinner with my mentor—an intuitive man who took me on at a time when I was a young graduate student and single mom in one of his research courses. He told me I had "that spark" and that he saw me doing something special with my life. We stayed in touch over the years, and he watched my journey—from the enthusiasm and hunger I had as a grad student to my decision to move clear across the country to marry Jackson years later.

That night at dinner, he said something that struck me. He said in all of those years that he had watched me grow and evolve, he observed with concern that even in all of that growth, I had almost lost my spark. I was still writing, still progressing, still succeeding, but for a time, I was doing all of that with a growing lack of passion.

How could this man see something in me from 2000 miles away that I could not see in myself? I had no idea that I was losing that spark he spoke of. As far as I was concerned, I had a newly minted Ph.D., I was presenting my research across the country, I was dabbling with teaching at the graduate level, and I had accomplished more than most people I knew at the time. How could any of that reveal a problem? Somehow, it did. I had become the crackhead—the one who thought if she dressed herself up, slapped on some sticky red lipstick, a wig, and a smile, no one would notice that there was a problem. But don't we always know a hardcore crackhead when we see one? I was that hardcore crackhead—not ill from crack, but ill from my relationship. Ill because I wasn't dealing with it. Ill because I figured everything would resolve itself over time.

My sister, if I didn't learn anything else over the last decade and a half of my life, I've learned this: bad relationships don't just resolve themselves over time. You have to address them. Slapping on your lipstick, a wig, and a smile does not make it go away. It makes you a crackhead. It deteriorates you. It eats away at you and your spark until both you and that spark are completely gone.

My mentor was right. I was losing it. I had reached a point of simply going through the motions. The worst of it was that final summer with Jackson. I spent those hot and humid months hiding under my covers. Literally. Even though I knew in my heart that he had been cheating, I never associated my state of being with my circumstances. If you had asked me what was wrong at the time, I honestly wouldn't have been able to tell you. I had resolved that I was experiencing extreme exhaustion—a delayed reaction from juggling my life with coursework and dissertation writing.

But this was not exhaustion. This was depression. It was much easier to chalk it all up to being really tired than it was to dig in and explore the true source of the pain. Too often, we dismiss what we are feeling as something else. We ignore it and allow our bodies to deteriorate because we don't want to face ourselves. I once knew a beautiful and sweet woman who died of cancer and had no idea she was so ill. Over the last few months of her life, she was dealing with such a high level of stress, she attributed her ailments to being busy and tired. By the time she found out what was really going on inside of her body, it was too late. She only had weeks to live. I don't mean to scare you or to sound overly dramatic, but this depression stuff is real. It can kill you if you turn a blind eye to it.

When I experienced it, I didn't know what to call it because depression was not something that was ever talked about in any of my circles—not among family, not among friends, not even at my job, even though I worked on a college campus as a student affairs professional. I was raised to believe that depression wasn't real—that it was just another word for weakness and defeat. We didn't air our dirty laundry. We didn't focus on our issues. If you were down about something, you were expected to pick yourself up and keep it moving. My family had a "suck it up" philosophy, so I learned to tell myself, *stop feeling sorry for yourself and get on with your life*. No differentiation was made between feeling momentarily sad and being genuinely depressed. We learned to suck it up and stop complaining.

That is the absolute wrong approach. I'm no medical doctor, but I do know that there are some basic signs of depression that you should be aware of and address. When someone who is going through a difficult time tells me that they spend most of their time in bed, are experiencing health problems, or that they have fantasized about "not being here" anymore, I ask them if they have considered the possibility of depression. Most of the time, the response is shock because it is not something they have considered. Sometimes, the response is "yes," and they have no idea what to do about it.

We've all heard of post-traumatic stress disorder (PTSD). This is a condition that our society seems to be much more aware of and sympathetic to. If you look at the symptoms, you'll notice that they are quite similar to the symptoms of depression, which, according to the American Psychological Association include:

- Difficulty concentrating, remembering details, and making decisions
- Fatigue and decreased energy
- Feelings of guilt, worthlessness, and/or helplessness
- Feelings of hopelessness and/or pessimism
- Insomnia, early-morning wakefulness, excessive sleeping
- Irritability, restlessness
- Loss of interest in activities or hobbies once pleasurable, including sex
- Overeating or appetite loss
- Persistent aches or pains, headaches, cramps, or digestive problems that do not ease even with treatment
- Persistent sad, anxious, or "empty" feelings
- Thoughts of suicide, suicide attempts

PTSD is similar, but has additional elements that include reliving the trauma, experiencing nightmares and hallucinations, and being fearful of settings that remind the victim of their trauma. What happens in the mind of a person who has experienced trauma directly affects the body. As is indicated in the list of symptoms above, depression after a breakup is no less detrimental to your physical health.

There is emerging about what is being called post-traumatic

growth. The basic idea is that after a traumatic situation, instead of deteriorating and falling victim to PTSD, there is another option—to experience post-traumatic growth. It means transforming that traumatic experience into a set of strategies and lessons that make your life better because of the strength and resilience gained after trauma. If this is possible after some of the most extreme forms of trauma, it is surely possible after the trauma of enduring a devastating breakup.

Getting yourself on the road to growth is precisely what I want you to accomplish as you work to heal your heart. *Growth.* But before you can experience that growth, it is essential that you address any unhealthy symptoms you may be experiencing. Do any of the above symptoms sound familiar to you? If any of them resonate with you, don't rule out the possibility of depression. If you ignore it, your symptoms will only get worse. The key is to know the symptoms. There were three basic symptoms that played out in my life: exhaustion, physical problems, and dark fantasies. I'll tell you about my experience. After that, I want you to consider what you can do to help yourself should depression come knocking on your door.

The Bed is My Refuge

I spent my last married summer in my bed. Not rolling under the covers in newlywed bliss or in warm embraces with the man I committed my life to. No, I was curled up in a fetal position. Hugging myself. Hiding. I wanted to shut the entire world out. My body was physically tired. It was an extreme case of exhaustion I had never experienced before. I literally couldn't drag myself out of bed unless I absolutely had to, and the longer I stayed in bed, the more exhausted I would become. The more exhausted I became, the more difficult it would be to get myself up. I wanted to be left alone. I didn't want to see anyone, talk to anyone, or look at anyone. It was too painful and took up too much energy to throw on my theatrical smile—my public face—only to return to my covers where I could strip back down to the lonely, zombie-like person I had become. I was a classic case of depression. I didn't know it. Jackson didn't know it. My loved ones didn't know it.

That loss of spark my mentor described was at the very depth of my depression. I was minimally functional. I did everything I needed to do as a wife, as a mom, and a scholar, but all with a mundane sense of routine and duty. I felt completely alone and guilty for not being the mom and wife I once I believed I could be. My kids didn't deserve this. I felt so guilty and lonely, I would often cry uncontrollably when no one was around. The weekdays were easier. On weekdays, I was able to hide behind the rigor of my daily routine. Get up, get the kids ready for day camp, drop everyone off, go to work, pick the kids up, keep them entertained, prepare dinner, get them ready for bed, then back under my covers. As long as I could follow that routine, I could fake being fine. Everything going on inside of me was undetectable.

Weekends were the worst. I dreaded them because there was no script. I would have to interact with Jackson and the kids casually and try not to be a drag. That never seemed to work. I found myself hiding under the covers every weekend, only coming out to go to church, to prepare meals, and to play mom when motherhood called. But even when motherhood called, I usually pretended to be asleep until Jackson stepped in. He was concerned at first, and he was always very helpful, but over time, I could tell that he was becoming increasingly annoyed. I didn't care what he thought. I couldn't move. I felt guilty every day. I wanted to be involved. I wanted to laugh. I wanted to be there for my kids in ways that I couldn't while I was in school, but I was stuck under those covers.

My Body Hurts

The longer I allowed myself to remain in my unhealthy situation, the more I deteriorated. I was physically ill. My young body responded over the years with ailments like arthritis, digestive problems, and weight gain. I lived years in a state of constipation, having no idea that my body was trying to tell me something. I actually believed that stomach pain after meals and only having a bowel movement once a week were normal. It wasn't until after I left Jackson that I realized how completely abnormal and unhealthy this was. I was so stressed out and depressed that everything inside of me literally clamped up.

On one morning I'll never forget, during one of the most stressful months of my life, my body decided that enough was enough. I was knee deep in doctoral work, was taking care of an infant and a pre-teen alone while Jackson traveled for work five days a week, and I worked in a toxic, unsupportive environment. There was no escaping the strain. Everywhere I turned I encountered a source of heartache. It all came to a head when I woke up one morning feeling a sensation of sharp pain in every joint in my body from my elbows to my fingers to my ankles to my knees. My body ached so severely that I could hardly walk. It was so sudden and unlike anything I had ever experienced. I ended up staying home from work that day to recover. The pain gradually eased over the course of the week, so I never went to see a doctor. At the time, I didn't associate my pain with the stress. Instead, I scoured the web to explore every possibility and draw every conclusion except the invisible, yet most obvious one—extreme stress.

Listen to your body. Your body is excellent at telling you if it is being abused. If you are constantly exhausted or have persistent health issues, your body may be trying to tell you something. Don't ignore it. There is a very special and real connection between what happens in your mind and in your body. If your mental state is unstable and unhealthy, your body will usually follow suit.

Dark Fantasies

I was screaming for help on the inside. I wanted to be rescued, but I didn't know what I wanted to be rescued from. When I looked at my life, even as a newlywed, everything appeared to be fine—nice house, husband, two kids, good job, great education. What was my problem? Was I ungrateful? I couldn't pinpoint it. All I knew was that sometimes, I just wanted to go to sleep and never wake up. There were times when I would be at work in such a state of sorrow and hopelessness that I would walk from meeting to meeting with my head down, watching my feet, legs feeling as light as the air, just praying that they would collapse under me so that I could crash to the ground. People would come to my rescue, and perhaps then, someone would know that I was not okay.

On my worst days, I fantasized about crashing my car into trees and flying over cliffs, just to entice the glorious lights and sirens of an ambulance. I fantasized about the heroic crew that would come running to untangle me and carry me away to safety. If I could be rescued, somehow, everything would be okay. You see, it wasn't that I wanted to actually die. I just wanted to be rescued. I wanted someone to save me because I had no idea how to save myself, and I had no idea what I needed to be saved from.

I never lived out my dark fantasies. Thankfully, I pulled through before any of them became my reality. I reached out for help to keep a level head. Reaching out saved my life. Had I stayed insulated in my own little world, there's no telling how far I would have descended into my downward spiral of depression. I reached out when I still had a flicker of spark left in me. When the first person I reached out to didn't respond, I reached out to someone else. I kept reaching until someone took my hand and I got what I needed.

Reach Out

Whatever you do, don't lose your spark. If you suspect that you are struggling with depression, even in the most minor sense, don't brush it off. Your health and your well-being are too important. Reach out before your spark goes out.

I know how difficult it can be to pull yourself out of the fog long enough to get help. The pride and the guilt and the fear of rejection can be enough to keep us in hiding. But trust me when I tell you that reaching out is well worth it. Start anywhere—with a life coach, a counselor, a family member, even a trusted friend. Reach out to anyone who will listen and has the ability to steer you in the right direction.

I am glad that I let Jackson go when I did. I can't imagine what would've happened had I chosen to stay and continued to swallow the pain. I sought help right away. I began meeting with Pastor Melva the week after I left him. And this is how I knew in hindsight that what I had been experiencing was indeed depression: everything felt better. For the first time that I remember, I was not constipated. I was regular! I no longer had episodes of arthritis pain. I started writing and pursuing my dreams again. I was able to laugh genuinely. I felt happiness that I hadn't felt in years. I had energy once again—a level of energy

I hadn't felt since college. I felt like myself. I had become the Pamela I hadn't known since I walked down the aisle.

Don't be too proud to ask for help. Your health is nothing to play with. Don't underestimate the power that depression can have over you if you let it. That thing affected every single aspect of my life, from my role as mother, to my performance at work, to my physical livelihood. It took over. The best way to defeat it is to first recognize it and then to take the step to do something about it. Pick up the phone and call someone. If that someone blows you off, call someone else. Keep reaching out until someone listens. Don't let anyone discourage you or tell you to suck it up. Don't give up on yourself, because I promise you, there is a better life on the other side of depression. You don't have to cry alone. No more hiding away. Find someone to talk to, so that you can get over this hump and keep your spark. You need that spark. Do what you must to keep it flickering.

Love you,

Dr. Pamela

CHAPTER THREE

REFOCUS YOUR PRIORITIES

Emptied
by Souldoll Love

My heart specializes in love.
The cross-eyed kind with red blinking lights, prescriptions,
and loads of sugar to patch up the rough spots.
The kind that uses cuss words to defend weaknesses and prayer to
stabilize lopsidedness.
I'm only human after all, so I refuse to walk you thru the warning
label
a fourth time again.
Providing proof of my loud bite may contradict your homemade
definitions of a lady,
So I mostly practice behind closing doors.
Not ashamed of being fragile until after I'm broken,
and who's gone love me now?
All covered in the make-beliefs of your scent,
Advertising the bruises of your disappointings,
Waiting in the web of your promise, legs crossed, clearin' my
throat, before proudly stating,
"It's all good Baby."
I've never looked good wearing disguises or background dancin'.
And pretending to only be pretending started wearin' me out,
So I decided to come clean.
Apologizing to God along the way.
Reviewing the script from the bottom up this time.
I always knew you'd show up with your fancy talk
and extra large expectations attached, requestin' the special...
Next time I'll politely turn my back and mumble
"Sorry, I'm fresh out."

Letter 9

A NEW LIFE ROUTINE

My Sister,

The most difficult part of letting go and moving on after Jackson was finding ways to fill the time I used to spend with him. He was a huge part of my life. We were family. We lived in the same house together. We spent a lot of time together. Even when times weren't the greatest, and our moments together were spent in anger, sadness, and frustration, it was time spent doing *something*. And in the end, I took comfort in knowing that even if the time wasn't enjoyable at the moment, it would eventually take a positive turn. Eventually. Even if just for a day. Isn't that crazy? I spent much of my time clinging to this belief that if I just put in the time, I would be rewarded. He will see me. He will love me. But I was never seen. And I was never loved the way I deserved to be. So, when it ended, I had to figure out what to do with all of that time and energy I was so used to spending on him.

But that's just me. Perhaps you weren't quite as hard-headed and obsessed with clinging to a belief as I was, but I am sure that before your relationship ended, you were probably consumed with trying to make it work. You probably stressed over it for awhile. And you probably didn't experience the kind of loneliness or boredom you may be feeling now.

Well, your life has changed. You've got a big empty space in the place where your ex once sat, and even if having them around was more miserable than blissful, that big empty space hurts. Be proactive about filling that space with something *healthy*. Not a random relationship. Not a bad habit. But something productive. Something that will add value to *you*. The trick is to identify those places in your life where you feel a void, and find ways to fill them with *purpose* and on purpose.

Changing your life takes strategy and deliberate action. I recommend that you begin with readjusting your daily routine and reprioritizing your life. If you were accustomed to chatting with your ex every morning at the start of your day, create a new tradition to fill that space and time. Choose something that puts a smile on your face. Take a yoga class in the mornings or have a good friend call you every morning as you're getting ready for your day. Meeting up with Najee for breakfast or lunch several times a week did wonders for keeping me in contact with another human being and allowing me to talk through what I was feeling.

If you lived together, this transition may be especially difficult. Going from our family home to an isolating apartment after leaving Jackson felt very drastic. One week, we were living in a neighborhood bustling with children, block parties, and music in the park across the street, and the very next week, my kids and I were in a quiet apartment complex where it seemed that every man for himself was the rule of the land. So, what did I do to fill some of the void? I stayed as busy as possible. I spent very little time sitting around in that apartment because I couldn't stand the fact that my daily routine as a wife came to a screeching halt. I mean, instantly. One day I was rushing home to cook dinner and do the evening family routine, and by the end of that day, I was packing my bags. Just like that. I had to quickly adjust and do what I could to keep moving forward.

Staying Busy

There was a point when I attended church four times a week to keep myself spiritually grounded—Monday night prayer, Wednesday night bible study, Saturday night service, and Sunday morning service. That helped tremendously. But I wanted to find some really *crazy* things to do that I had never tried before. So on Wednesday nights, I went to church, and on Thursday nights, just for a little contrast and a lot of fun, I went to a pole-dancing class. Yes, pole-dancing! And yes...*by myself*! Of course, there was a room full of other women who attended for their own reasons—college girls who went in girlfriend packs (I kind of envied them), married women who wanted to seduce their husbands, fitness gurus who saw this as a fun way to stay in shape, and then little ole me—a newly single woman who just needed to get out of the house and break out of her shell by trying something new. Honestly, I didn't do a whole lot of breaking out of my shell in that class, as it never ceased to be totally embarrassing, but it certainly was a whole lot of fun and kept me from sinking into a well of self-pity and misery—on Thursday nights, anyway.

I kept my schedule packed. I played tennis before church on Wednesdays and Saturdays, and I started working out daily—for stress relief. I took piano lessons on Monday afternoons, and once a month, a girlfriend and I joined a group of women from her job to play Bunco—a game I had never heard of but came to thoroughly enjoy.

As a mother of two, I certainly needed and *loved* my quiet time, but I refused to allow myself to spend too much time alone—until I reached a point where being alone was no longer a sure path to agony. I had completely rearranged my daily and weekly routine in response to the changes that had occurred in my life. Yes, I had a toddler and a pre-teen to care for, and yes, I still had a full-time job, but as soon as my marriage ended, I decided that my peace of mind and my health were a priority, and that I could not function as a competent mother if I was falling to pieces every day. So I figured out how to do what was necessary to take care of my kids and myself at the same time.

But as I was going to church and swinging on poles and exchanging cookie recipes with my sisterhood of Bunco women, I knew that I still had some "stuff" to deal with. It would have been really easy for me to stay *so* busy that I ignored what was really going on in my life. And that would have been tragic because it would have meant that I was doing all of this running around in vain. The reality is, at the end of each day, I had to face myself and my situation. I was in the midst of a divorce. My relationship failed. My fairy tale didn't end happily ever after. I had done everything possible to make it right, and it still failed. No matter how busy I kept myself, this truth wasn't going anywhere. I had to deal with it. So, what did I do on Tuesday nights? Therapy.

Yes, *me*. A Black woman who went against the unwritten rules of all of the strong silently hurting women in my family. Yep. I did it. I went to therapy. I had been seeing Pastor Melva for spiritual guidance, and she was awesome, but she had a church to run and certainly didn't have time to meet with me on a weekly basis. I needed to check in with someone regularly to ensure that I was okay, that I was on track. I *felt* okay. I hadn't had any major breakdowns since leaving Jackson, I had long abandoned my dark fantasies, and I didn't turn to alcohol or drugs. I felt pretty stable—as long as I stayed busy. But I didn't trust how good I was feeling. I wanted to be sure that I wasn't faking myself out (the women in my family do this exceptionally well), so I met with a therapist once a week who kept me in check and challenged me to keep thinking about my next steps in life.

While engaging in this crazy new routine of mine, I chose to stay connected to my reality through my therapist and my pastor. You may choose to do it differently. It doesn't matter how you address it. Just be sure that you do, because if you don't, as soon as you get sick of your busy routine and begin to slow your life down, you'll look up and get slapped with the reality that your life has drastically changed. That will either hit you like a ton of bricks or it will cause you to dance for joy. Obviously, the latter would be great, but you certainly don't want to wake up a year from now buried under a ton of bricks because you lived on pure denial all year. Stay busy, readjust your routine to accommodate the changes, and make sure you're *addressing* what is happening in your life.

If you're not sure how to develop this new routine, start by making a list of all of the things you've always wanted to do (a bucket list, as they say), and try to do what you can. If you aren't sure how to make connections, the internet is a great resource. Meetup.com is an example of a site that connects groups of people by their interests. For example, if you'd like to find a group of Bunco women, a book club, a girlfriends' travel group, or even a women's full-contact football team to join (no joke!), you may be able to find it there. There are mommy and me groups. Singles groups. Business networking groups. If you sign up for several, you'll end up with more opportunities to network and play than you may be able to handle. And that's a good thing! You don't have to participate in all of them, but at least give yourself some options.

After you've made your list and have sought out the opportunities in your area, start mapping out your new routine—how you'll spend each day—Monday through Sunday. And in your plan, don't forget to include some *keepin' it real* time in order to come face to face with the reality of your situation. For some, keeping a journal is helpful. For others, talking it out works. For me, a combination of both was most effective.

Changing your routine is an important step to refocusing your life. In my next letter, I'll provide some insight about refocusing your priorities.

Love you lots!

Dr. Pamela

♥ INSPIRE YOUR HEART

Think about some ways you can change your routine from day to day:

	My Old Routine	My New Routine
Monday		
Tuesday		
Wednesday		
Thursday		
Friday		
Saturday		
Sunday		

My Strategies For:

Meeting new people

Addressing childcare issues

Finding new activities

Finding time around my work schedule

Letter 10

SLIDING BACKWARDS

My Sister,

I know that this letter is supposed to be about changing your priorities, but first, I thought we should pause for a second. I need to check in with you to see how you've been doing. Letting go is not an easy process. You probably have great days and then really crappy days. Sometimes, you may see a future full of possibilities ahead of you, and other times, nothing. The future feels just plain hopeless. That's how I felt in my lowest moments. Even the best of us slip up from time to time. There are no guarantees that each of these strategies will work perfectly every time. Letting go is a complex process. It doesn't often come easy. Challenges weren't designed that way. They have this knack for catching you off guard.

The reality of it all is that these are strategies, and we are *human*. Those human emotions and fears and insecurities that we're so blessed to have are very real. They're unpredictable. They're overwhelming. And they can strike in some of the most inopportune times. When this happens, you may be tempted to slide backwards and pick up the phone or convince yourself that it is not *really* over.

Sliding backwards is like climbing a mountain and suddenly realizing halfway up that you're afraid of heights. Or maybe finding yourself overcome with the fear of what may be waiting for you at the top. Perhaps you long for the stability of feeling level ground under your feet. In a panic, you stop and lose your balance and find yourself slipping—sliding backwards, undoing the progress you made to get to where you are. When we slide backwards, we lose our bearings. We succumb to fear and begin to question our faith. *Did I really make the right decision here? What if I'm still single five years from now? Twenty years from now?! What have I done? How could I ever feel just as comfortable, or as great, or as compatible with anyone other than them? Maybe I overreacted. Maybe we just didn't try hard enough. Maybe they've changed the way they feel and miss me too but don't know how to say it. Maybe I can help them find the words.*

After having this conversation with yourself long enough, after going through the pictures and the letters, and after checking their Facebook profile a gazillion times, you decide that you *must* do something. Anything. But something. So, you pick up the phone and call, or whip together a nifty, carefully worded email or text message just to connect once more, to feel them out, to see if they respond. This is not letting go. This is sliding backwards.

Have you been there yet? Not all of us do it, but many are at least tempted. My problem is that when I'm tempted to do something that I really want to do, I shove all voices of reason aside and dive in head-first. *Shut up, I'm going in!* This, more often than not, is disastrous.

So how, exactly, do you avoid sliding backwards? It's important to know when you're most vulnerable to giving in to these sliding moments. We all have triggers—times in our lives or certain events that make dealing with the loss of a relationship even more unbearable than usual.

My Sliding Backwards Moment

I slid down my slippery slope during the month of December. Najee and I were on a "time-out" because I had proposed that we not talk for awhile. I was having a hard time with the fact that he wanted to be no more than friends. He agreed to the time-out. We couldn't have picked a worse time to come up with this agreement. December—a month consisting of both Christmas and my birthday. Between trying to savor what I could for my birthday—alone—and tolerating the rest of the world's grand celebrations of Christmas and Hanukkah and Kwanzaa that month, I was constantly reminded of the fact that I wasn't sharing any of this with anyone. I didn't have a special "boo" to take me out for an unforgettable birthday. There would be no cold December nights cuddling next to the warm fireplace (not that I had a fireplace, but it was worth the fantasy, right?).

The worst part of it all? The questions from random, well-meaning people. The endless *what are you doing for your birthday* and *are you ready for Christmas* questions. I was lonely in a new city with no friends, and my kids were both with their dads, so any impressive answers I came up with would have been nothing short of lies. Those questions were just enough to keep me angry and resentful of everyone else's bliss throughout the entire month. It was all I could do to just get to January. *For God's sake, please just get me to January!*

In my eyes, of course, everyone else's life was perfect. With Christmas songs everywhere, houses cheerfully decorated, and families planning grand get-togethers, all I could think about was that *my* family was in pieces. My family no longer existed. And then, on top of everything else, I couldn't even have Najee, because in his words, "timing is everything." *What the heck does timing have to do with anything? Is love not greater than timing? How could he let me be alone?* I was so angry with him, I became consumed with my loneliness. I stopped thinking about the big picture. I lost sight of my ultimate goal, which was to get my life back together.

I felt myself slowly losing grasp of all rational thinking on one particular day while wandering around in Target during the height of the holiday season. I was having a mental meltdown. Christmas shopping was in full swing. People were bumping into me. A child was screaming. The checkout lines spilled deep into the aisles. The world was spinning twice as fast that day, I was sure of it. My thoughts were consumed with Najee. At any moment, I was going to lose my mind. *Why won't this man just love me?!* I had all of this emotion ready to burst out of me, and amazingly, it never seemed to occur to *anyone* that I was trying my very best to hold it all together and not have a breakdown in the middle of that crowded, festive store. *Does nobody in this world feel my pain?* I felt so alone. All I really wanted from Target that day was a freakin' Ghirardelli's chocolate caramel bar to melt some of the misery away. That was it. No Christmas presents. No wrapping paper. Just candy. *Just give me the chocolate bar (and a side order of Najee). Please!*

This is where the internal dialogue of craziness really began. I was slipping. Because at that point, I just didn't care anymore. *How much worse can it get? What was I thinking suggesting a time-out? For Najee and I not to be talking, especially during this time of year, is just stupid. This is stupid. Oh...I'll just call him.*

And there I went. Sliding backwards fast. As that familiar sharp stone grazed my hip on my way down the rugged hill of progress, I suddenly remembered why I didn't want to return to that place. *Ouch!* But it was too late. The damage was done. I called him. I lost all sense of control. I whined about how much I missed him. I cried. I apologized. And then...I listened to his silent disappointment on the other end of the phone. Instantly, I felt like an idiot.

You know what's so horrible about sliding backwards? You think you're doing something that will make you feel better, but mark my words: you will *not* feel better after the slide! If this is a situation in which you know in your heart that it is time to move on, sliding backwards will only complicate things. It will make you feel worse. It will open up a can of worms that shouldn't be opened, and it may undo the progress that you've made thus far.

When I broke down and called Najee that December, just two days before Christmas, I learned that he was not nearly as distraught about our time-out as I had been. In fact, he was doing a fine job of moving on, complete with holiday plans and a renewed optimism about how this coming year would be the best of his life. *Perfect.* Not having me around actually seemed to be somewhat of a relief for him. I felt like a ball of crap and sorely regretted my decision to make that phone call. I had almost made it to January, and then somehow, couldn't resist the urge.

I was vulnerable. This was a difficult time of year for me, and I was not prepared for how it would hit me. I had nothing in place to lift my spirits or buffer my strength. When you hit these vulnerable moments, extra doses of support are paramount. Be sure to take precautions and get your ducks (or friends) lined up to help keep you moving. But you have to be able to swallow your pride. I'm not saying that everyone needs to know that you're about to hit a rough patch, but I do recommend enlisting one or two trusted and loyal friends to be on alert for your well-being.

When I finally opened up and told one of my friends about how this month was a struggle for me, he was more than willing to be a source of refuge. "When you feel the need to call him, call me instead. I will make myself available." I *so* wish I had reached out sooner so that I could have been armed with this type of support well before the end of December. I hadn't told anyone about my struggle until shortly *after* my sliding moment to gripe about how weak and stupid I was.

Give Yourself Grace

And that brings me to my final point. You are *not* weak and stupid. You are human. With real feelings, real emotions, and real insecurities. If you ever slide backwards in a large or small way, if you ever become overwhelmed with the temptation to slide backwards, this does not mean that you are weak or stupid. Don't be too hard on yourself. The last thing you need is to get down on yourself in the midst of this very difficult life transition. This, my sister, is not an easy process, and much of it is about learning and figuring it out as you go. So, nobody (not even me!) will go through this perfectly and gracefully. We may be clumsy, speechless, compulsive, annoying, and unorthodox through it all, but as long as we are getting *through* it, it will all come together eventually. You'll make mistakes. *You will.* Just dust yourself off and learn from them so that you'll be smarter and wiser next time. And if you're seeing a therapist, counselor, or spiritual mentor, don't be too embarrassed to tell them about the mistakes and these moments of sliding backwards. They can help you process why you went there and how to avoid going there again.

Be sure that you're aware and not caught off guard. Think about scenarios, events, and moments in which you may be vulnerable enough to slide backwards. Then, come up with a game plan for how you will get your extra dose of support during those times. At the very least, you will be aware and ready when and if that temptation starts to creep in. I hope this helps you, Sis. In my next letter, we'll talk about reprioritizing for sure. Promise!

Love you,

Dr. Pamela

Letter 11

NEW LIFE
NEW PRIORITIES

My Sister,

In the prime of my time with Najee, he was one of my greatest priorities. Everything I did, I did with him in mind. My hair, my nails, my outfit, even my grocery shopping. I wanted to know what he liked to eat, how he liked it cooked, and what made him smile, because if it made him smile, I wanted to do it. I bounced every major decision I needed to make off of him. I developed a love for music and fashion and football and boxing because of him. He opened up my world to so much that I had never experienced. My life became fully consumed with my love and admiration for him. If he wasn't in my presence, he was on my mind. He was in my heart. He was always with me. Yes, girl. I was *all the way* gone. He was my world and the only future I could see.

Wanting Najee to be happy and satisfied was a priority for me, and I was more than pleased to oblige. I don't regret it. It was awesome while it lasted, and I learned a great deal about myself. One of the most important lessons I learned was about the importance of *paying attention*. While I was allowing myself to be consumed with all of the giving and loving and pleasing, I stopped paying attention to where he was in all of this. Najee was a huge priority in my life, and while I was important to him, he certainly never placed me on the type of pedestal I had placed him upon. He was more focused on other aspects of his life. I wasn't paying attention. He actually told me on many occasions that a relationship was not ideal for either of us at this point in our lives. Each time he gently reminded me of this, I covered my ears tightly and began to sing love songs to myself—very loudly. Well...not literally, but I definitely wasn't listening.

Now, of course, when I look back upon that glorious year, our mismatched priorities are so abundantly obvious. It explains why my friends and family kept telling me to be careful. But if you haven't figured this out about me by now, I'm a pretty hard-headed and strong-willed woman, as I have been called. I don't always listen. I do what I want to do the way I want to do it. These two qualities often work in my favor because when I set my mind to something, I usually get it done. But these qualities have also backfired on me because they don't usually work well when I try to impose what I want upon another unwilling party. Sometimes, I *refuse* to learn by listening. I usually opt to bang my own head against the wall a few times to see for myself that forehead against brick does indeed hurt. So even though all of those people were absolutely right, at that point in my life, I was not going to be satisfied until I saw it, felt it, and tasted it for myself. And boy did I.

My point is that Brian, Jackson, and Najee were all major priorities in my life. They were everything, and then suddenly, they were gone. I had to reprioritize quickly. All of those things I used to do with them in mind, I needed to do for a new purpose. No longer for them, but for me, which is probably how it should have been in the first place.

Here's another important lesson that I learned: Never lose yourself for the sake of clinging to someone else, especially if you are not as high on his priority list as he is on yours. Keep this in mind as you reprioritize your life. This is a great opportunity to make *yourself* a priority if you are not already.

I recommend that you take this ex of yours, who was once a major priority in your life, and move them off of the priority list altogether. Yes, *off* the list. Even if the two of you remain friends down the line, today they need to come off the priority list for your sake. Today, you are in the midst of healing, working on letting go, and working towards bringing peace and order to your life. It's counterproductive to attempt to do this while still trying to be their friend or looking out for their well-being.

Don't get me wrong. I'm not saying that your ex has to be completely shut out of your life. Shutting Brian and Jackson out was not an option because we each have a child together. We will always be connected in that sense. Because of that, I made it a point never to disrespect either of them, but I also stopped taking responsibility for their needs. My priorities were the needs of our child and myself, and these needs are what have guided how I have chosen to interact with them.

Regardless of what your connection with your ex will be today, tomorrow, or years to come. I recommend taking them off of your priority list as you go through this transition. Today, *you* are your priority. What will it take to make you feel more fulfilled, complete, and even happy with where you are heading in life? That is how you determine what should be a priority.

In the past, your relationship was a priority because it was what you thought might be a very important component of your future, and because your ex was one of those people in your life you cared deeply about. Now that your future has a different (and better) outlook, you have one less highly important person in your life. This means that some of your time and energy is freed up and can be applied to other aspects of your life that may have been neglected. What have you spent less time focusing on since meeting your ex? Loved ones? A dream? An old hobby? Your health? Now is the time to reprioritize and decide what you will pay special attention to.

When I was with Jackson, I neglected three particular areas in my life that were once huge priorities for me: writing, working out regularly, and bonding with friends. Of course, I'm the one responsible for neglecting those things. This was so indicative of how much of myself I was willing to sacrifice and pay less attention to in exchange for meeting his needs. After leaving him, the things I neglected became painfully obvious because without him around, I finally took the time to look at myself. Not only did I not recognize myself, I didn't even recognize where I was! *How the heck did I end up here? I was supposed to be a writer, an author, an anchorwoman, a talk show host. And what am I doing in the Midwest?* No wonder I was so miserable and unfulfilled. Who was this person I had become?

I made a vow to myself never to neglect what I love again, particularly because these specific things—writing, working out, and bonding with friends—were important to me. I decided that if ever again I get so consumed with someone that I begin to neglect what I treasure, that person simply is not the one for me. With the right guy, I will not be less of myself. I will actually be more of myself. I will not only continue to write, exercise, and socialize, but I will thrive in those areas with him in my life. He will appreciate that part of me. What I love to do will be important to him because they're important to me, and he will encourage me to do more of it and to do it well.

Do you see what a great opportunity you have at this point in your life to check and rearrange your priorities? You can use this time to look back (reflect upon what you may have neglected), to look at today (recognize what you will make a priority), and to look at tomorrow (prepare for your future).

In order to determine what your priorities are or should be, ask yourself what was important to you before the relationship started. What do you miss that you stopped doing while you were with your ex? Who have you missed and need to reconnect with? What goals did you let go of that you would still like to accomplish? What have you been slacking on that you would like to improve?

But let's not be all gloom and doom about this. There must be something good that came from your time in that relationship—some good habits developed, some new aspects of yourself discovered. I can think of several things I picked up from my marriage that I still consider to be a priority today. Ideally, when a relationship ends, all is not lost, and we have become enriched and wiser as a result of the experience. Before I got married, for example, I loved to cook, but never spent much time in the kitchen. After I married, I made it a point to cook every night. I loved it. It was a creative outlet for me that I continued to pursue even after the marriage ended. Think about what your relationship helped you develop and decide whether or not these are qualities you want to keep on your list of priorities.

And then...there are those habits you developed that you may want to purge—those things that you started doing as a result of the relationship that you want to take off of your priority list. Perhaps you started smoking or drinking more. Maybe you left your church to join theirs, or maybe you eliminated pork from your diet because they did. Whatever it is, if it is something that was more important to you within the context of the relationship than it is now that you are single, consider taking it off of your priority list. If it is something you'd like to abandon, something you did half-heartedly to satisfy or impress your ex, or something you did to keep the peace, consider dropping it. Even if you don't want to neglect it completely, you certainly have the liberty to determine the level of importance these new habits will have in your life. Let's say you *like* the no pork idea but want to build in some exceptions. Or you actually like their religious denomination but would prefer not attending their church. Do your thing, girl! You're in the driver's seat.

The point is that your ex is no longer a priority of yours. You can redesign your life and your priorities as you choose. You can wisely use this time to examine your past decisions and determine who you are and what is important today. Then, you can build the parameters for the next relationship around this new understanding of who you are and what's important to you. If you commit to standing firm in who you are, you'll never again have to sacrifice and lose yourself for fear of losing the relationship. I mean, really, if you lose someone as a result of holding on to what you value, that someone never fully embraced you to begin with. Let them go. It's all a part of life's natural process of elimination. Don't fight it. Go with it. There are bigger fish in the sea. That, I know for sure!

Love,

Dr. Pamela

♥ INSPIRE YOUR HEART

On the Priority List	Off the Priority List

CHAPTER FOUR

REFOCUS YOUR GOALS

Love Has Spoken
By Khari Lemuel
Music & Self-Mastery

Stop walking round here unprepared.
Stop being scared.
Stop doing all the crazy things you do.
That ain't you.
Stop wasting precious time you have
Complainin' 'bout your circumstance,
Believing that you're what you're going through.
That ain't you.
Don't you remember who you are?
Don't you remember?
And even after all this time
Please tell me why you don't know what you're here to do.

Did you know that when I made you, you were pure love?
Did you know that when I made you, you were whole?
Did you know that you were born of pure divinity,
A true mystery to unfold?

Fill your heart with love, let go of hate.
Focus your mind and concentrate.
Create yourself and start your life anew.
And I guarantee the moment that you do,
You'll introduce yourself to you.

Did you know that when I made you, you were pure love?
Did you know that when I made you, you were whole?
Did you know that you were born of pure divinity,
A true mystery to unfold?

Share your world and don't you hesitate.
Focus your mind and meditate.
Don't be afraid to let the light shine through.
And I guarantee the moment that you do,
You'll introduce yourself to you.

Letter 12

YOUR SELF-IMPROVEMENT GOAL

My Sister,

Let's talk about your goals! I'm talking about a firm set of goals that you've set for yourself, separate from anything related to your ex; those goals that have the potential to propel you into the life you've always dreamed of living; goals that keep you in check so that you always have something to work toward. If you haven't defined your goals (or if you need a fresh new set), there's no better time than the present to get some established. In the next few letters, we'll focus on setting at least four goals: a self-improvement goal, a strength goal, a professional goal, and a spiritual goal. Setting goals has dual benefits. It distracts you from the heartbreak, and it gives you the opportunity to focus on enhancing your life.

After I left Jackson, the very first thing I did was set some goals for myself. I knew that I had a lot of work to do and that the next year would be a challenging one, so I decided to keep myself preoccupied with self-improvement tasks. My first order of business, after both Brian and Jackson, was to uncover aspects of myself that brought me into those unhealthy relationships to begin with. Those were the aspects that I needed to change. My primary issue, I discovered, was that I was too passive.

I can recall quite vividly one night when Brian had picked a fight with me for no apparent reason. He left my apartment in a rage, refusing to tell me where he was going. After several hours of not hearing from him, I got into my car and drove to the place where my instincts led me—his ex-girlfriend's house. Sure enough, there parked in her driveway at one a.m. was his rusty 1974 Monte Carlo. Trying to collect my thoughts, I parked across the street, unsure of what to do. I was five months pregnant with a newly visible baby bump, so I couldn't do anything too stupid...but I had to do something.

I sat in my car for about five minutes trying to clear my head before a woman came storming out of the front door of the house. She walked heavily down the walkway toward my car with Brian trailing behind her. I could hear her cursing. I got out of my car and walked across the street toward her, not sure of what would happen. I was surprised by my own boldness. This woman, who seemed to be at least five years older than me, was visibly angry. We stood in the middle of the street about five feet away from one another as she continued to scream about what the hell I was doing at her house. But I wasn't focused on her. My eyes were fixated on Brian. She was ready for a fight, lunging at me several times as Brian worked to hold her back. I didn't flinch, but I also didn't say much. I stood there stunned. Without looking at her, I asked him, "So, this is what you want, Brian?"

He looked at me with a coldness I will never forget. "Yeah," he said with a nod that seemed to be more reassuring for himself than for me. "Yeah, this is what I want."

Without another word, I took a deep breath and returned to my car, with his lady of choice still screaming at my back. In her eyes, she had won. They remained in the middle of the street as I drove myself and my precious baby bump away from that scene. I held it together just long enough to get out of his sight before I began sobbing uncontrollably.

Some may say that my response that night wasn't passive, but dignified. Perhaps. But the dignity didn't last long. Passivity kicked in when Brian called me the next day to apologize and I took him back without hesitation. Yes, I did. This was the pattern of our relationship. I knew how to flee a standoff and declare "it's over!" after he disrespected me, but I didn't know how to stick to my guns and stand up for myself once the dramatic dust had settled.

Had I been more assertive in my relationships with Brian and Jackson, I wouldn't have dealt with so much drama over the years. If I had stood my ground about what my needs were, one of two things would've happened in each case: the relationship would have improved, or it would have dissolved much sooner and spared us both some pain.

It's important to acknowledge your own role in the failure of the relationship (no matter how perfect you think you were or how awful you think that other person may have been). If you don't, it will be impossible to learn from the experience and to apply that knowledge the next time around. When I was walking away from Jackson, for example, after dwelling on all the ways he had let me down, I began to reflect on my own actions and decisions. I asked myself what it was about me that allowed things to go the way that they did. *What could I have done differently? What do I not want to repeat once I step into a new relationship?*

The answer was loud and clear: I didn't know how to stand up for myself. In my relationships with Brian and Jackson, I had allowed these guys to get comfortable with my tendency not to speak up for myself and to hide how serious, hurt, or angry I was. I was so good at being even-tempered and calm that through my calmness (and sometimes passivity), I led them to believe that they could have their way in the relationship, even if it meant disrespecting me.

Let me be clear. I am not giving them a pass for this behavior. No man of integrity should allow himself to fall that deeply into a pattern of disrespect. It is very important, however, to be honest with yourself and to take responsibility for your own contribution to the issue no matter how small it was. You don't want to find yourself in the same place this time next year. Think about it. What would you do differently from the moment you met him, to the moment you first opened up, to the moment you realized that it was going downhill? What stands out most to you?

Take time between now and a year from today to set a new course for your life. As you stand at this at this crossroads, you have an amazing opportunity take a different direction in life—to experience joy, success, and fulfillment. I suggest that you take one or two of your most obvious issues (we've all got them), and turn them into goals. The issue I most wanted to change after leaving Jackson was my tendency to be overly passive, so my first goal was to become more assertive over the course of that year. As I spent more time focusing on this goal, I realized that my passivity was not just evident in my romantic relationships, but also in my interactions with classmates in graduate school and colleagues at work. This critical discovery compelled me to take a more empowering stance within each of my relationships.

We all can use some work in particular areas to improve ourselves. As you go through this transition in your life, consider what you can do to take yourself to the next level.

What will it take to avoid falling into or continuing a pattern of unhealthy relationships? When you identify the personal issue that you will work on over the next year, you may discover that this very issue also shows up in your other relationships— perhaps among colleagues, friends, family members, or even strangers. It'll pay off big time to resolve it once and for all. It definitely takes time and effort, but if you stick with your plan, you'll reap the benefits of improving in numerous areas of your life.

Love,

Dr. Pamela

♥ INSPIRE YOUR HEART

1. What role did I play in the decline of this relationship? What important lessons did I learn about myself?

2. What personality trait do I struggle with that can use some improvement?

3. My self-improvement goal is to do what over the course of the next year?

Letter 13

YOUR STRENGTH GOAL

My Sister,

Now that you've identified a self-improvement goal, let's look at your strengths. This next goal is intended to further develop a strength that you can take to the next level. Your strength goal will balance out your self-improvement goal by helping you focus on building up a part of yourself that shows some great potential.

My strength has always been in my writing. Writing is a talent and a passion that I've had for as long as I could remember. When I write, I am at ease. I don't doubt myself. It's my thing. My educational path and career stem from my love for writing. Some of the most crucial moments of my life have been documented by my writing, which has served as an outlet to process my emotions, my fears, and my life aspirations. Writing is the way I communicate with the people I love when I'm too flustered to talk. It's the way I sort out my thoughts and visualize my dreams. Writing is the one area in my life for which I have received the most praise—from my parents, teachers, colleagues, and peers—all confirming for me that writing is more than something that I just like to do. It is something that I was born to do. But what I realized is that throughout the course of my marriage, the time I spent developing and nurturing this strength had diminished significantly. So, it wasn't difficult for me to resolve that my second goal—my strength goal—should be to focus on establishing my craft as a writer.

My writing goal had two parts. The first part was more abstract: to work on my craft as a writer by writing more frequently. The second part was more practical: to complete at least one writing project that I will submit for publication within a year. This gave me an actual project to work on, which totally consumed me at times. If I wasn't busy enough before, this goal surely kept my mind off of my losses and on my journey to the future. I developed a commitment to writing as if it were my new boyfriend. I'd take my notebook to restaurants, to parks, and even church. I'd sit in the empty sanctuary after service and just write what was on my heart. Wherever I went, my notebook went with me, and before long, I had fully reconnected with my old writing self. In fact, I was even better and more committed than I was many years before. The more I wrote, the better I got.

What about you? What do you passionately miss doing as a single woman? What strength or talent have you neglected that you can spend time focusing on? If you can't think of anything, try borrowing some clues from your childhood. What did you enjoy doing as a child that you may be able to revisit and reclaim as an adult? Were you a dancer? Did you play soccer? Were you in the drama club? Was it fashion design? Electronics? Photography? Perhaps there is something you've never tried but always knew you'd be good at, like mountain climbing, public speaking, or jewelry making. If you're still having a hard time figuring it out, ask an old friend, a sibling, a cousin— someone who has known you for a long time. Often these people can quickly pinpoint something about who you are that you hadn't noticed.

Spending your time perfecting a skill that you're good at helps to lift your self-esteem and confidence. I remember how much time I spent just after my marriage ended replaying all that I could have done differently. I remember how devastating it felt not to be able to get Jackson to treat me the way I wanted to be treated. In my lowest moments, I found myself questioning whether or not I had been good enough to get what I wanted out of the relationship. *Had I not done all of the right things? Was I not fulfilling enough?* But the moment I started to focus on what I enjoy, my outlook on everything changed. I began to hold my head up high, and I remembered who I was before my self-esteem began to dwindle during my time in the marriage.

The other benefit of spending time doing what you're good at is simple: you get better at it. If you take it seriously enough, it can become your bread and butter. What could be better than spending your time doing something that you're good at— something that makes you feel good about yourself—and getting paid for it? But whether or not you get paid, when you immerse yourself in something that you're good at, you are refocusing. The more you focus on developing your gifts, the less you'll obsess over that relationship that didn't work.

Well, my sister, I'm going to wrap this letter up and give you something to chew on before I give you the last few tidbits on refocusing your goals. Between this and my next letter, I want you to really think about what skill you might want to spend the next year perfecting. When you figure out what that is, challenge yourself. Set a specific goal that will encourage you to put that skill into action, and then get busy. If it's jewelry making, for example, set a date and location for when and where you will display and sell your collection. Don't be too hard on yourself.

Don't pull back out of fear or require that you achieve perfection. Just do *something* and look forward to basking in the glory of your accomplishment. I know that you can make it happen, because you're amazing like that.

Love you,

Dr. Pamela

♥ **INSPIRE YOUR HEART**

What strengths do I have?

Which of these will I focus on developing over the next year?

What specific goals do I aim to accomplish while using this strength?

Letter 14

YOUR PROFESSIONAL GOAL

My Sister,

Oh, the roller coaster of emotions I experienced each time my heart was broken! My moods were unpredictable from one moment to the next. One day, I hated him. The day after that, I was devastated. Often, I'd find myself angry for the unfair turn of events that resulted in my new status as "single." And then I'd have good days. Great days. Days when I would hear a song like Destiny Child's "Independent Woman" or Christina Aguilera's "Fighter" and I'd be the strongest, most confident, and most powerful woman in the world.

What's interesting is that my great days weren't based on a hate or a disdain for my exes, but in a newfound ever-growing love for myself—an appreciation for the lessons I've learned, and an internal strength that I never realized I had. Yes, there were great days—and what I learned was that those days were brought on by my ability to refocus. Focusing on my goals was an important step to seeing *more* great days, and I found that the more I focused on improving myself, the more great days I was able to enjoy. This is what I want for you, Sis—more great days.

We've looked at two types of goals you can set as part of your refocusing process. The first goal was self-improvement.

The second was developing your strengths. Now, let's think about something you can do to advance yourself professionally. Let's face it. Financial stability is a basic need we will always want to maintain. Why not focus on strengthening yourself as a professional? It doesn't matter what you currently do for a living, but it *is* important to know what you would like to be doing eventually and set a goal that would place you on the road to getting there. This goal does not have to be a difficult or time-consuming one. It doesn't even have to be directly related to your ultimate career goal. Maybe you have no clue what your ultimate career goal is. If that is the case, I would encourage you to set a general goal that could improve you professionally in any field that you decide to pursue.

If you are already exactly where you want to be professionally, that's awesome! You're the envy of many women I know. But don't stop there. It is never good to become so content with where you are that you become complacent and cease to grow. It is important to stay fresh, current, and competitive. What can you do that will keep you fresh and current? What will make you better and even more competitive than you are now? Take those things and work them into a goal to focus on over the next year.

Just as my marriage was on the verge of ending, I began to realize that I was climbing up the wrong professional ladder. I was working at a reputable university in student affairs with my eyes set on ascending to the vice president's office. Yet, I was miserable in my role. The profession and the work environment did not fit my personality or accentuate my strengths, and I knew that a promotion or more money would not have alleviated my misery. I wanted to pursue another career path—as a university professor—and I was finishing up a degree that would allow me to do just that.

At that point in my life, I had to consider what skills I could develop that would make me a stronger professional in my current role as an assistant dean, as well as prepare me for the role I desired to have as a graduate-level professor. As a proud introvert, I knew that I wasn't the greatest at networking. I had a bad case of social anxiety. I felt awkward in professional social settings—to the point where I dreaded them! *What am I supposed to say? How do I strike up conversation with this random person?* Clearly, if I wanted to be successful, I needed to resolve this issue. So that became my goal. I decided to *force* myself to network more until I felt comfortable with it. I asked people who were masters of networking to teach me their strategies. I became a student of the networking craft over the next year, doing whatever was necessary to get better at it. And because I continued to work at it, I did get better over the course of that year.

I challenge you to do the same. Think about what you can do to enhance yourself professionally. It may be a very specific goal, such as taking courses to get certified in a new field. You may even set a more general goal that can benefit your personal *and* professional life, such as improving your conflict resolution skills. Perhaps you want to pursue a degree that will make you more marketable in your current position. Maybe you have always wanted to spearhead a new initiative within your organization. What steps can you take to make that new initiative happen?

Your professional development goal creates a win-win situation for you. It helps to develop yourself at a time when it's easy to allow your job to suffer. It helps to build up your sense of competence when you feel compelled to question your value and worth. And it keeps your mind on the positive aspects of your life at a time when it seems more logical to focus on the negative and what is no longer there. Enhancing yourself professionally keeps you focused on moving forward. When we're going through difficult moments in our lives and it appears that time has just stood still, or that these miserable moments simply will not pass, it's helpful to look ahead and use the future as a focal point. Where would you like to be? How would you like to feel? Focus on getting to that place, rather than dwelling on where you are today.

Easier said than done? It is. But it's also doable. Achieving your goals takes strategy, discipline, and perseverance. I didn't have these qualities at first, but it didn't mean that I was excused from having to be strategic, disciplined, and persevering if I expected to get to where I wanted to be. I had to suck it up and do what I didn't really want to do. I had to stretch myself even when I didn't feel like it. There were no shortcuts in getting to the finish line. It hurt, but it was the kind of hurt you feel after working out for the first time in ages. The kind of hurt that says *my muscles ache because I am being really productive. I'm moving and bending in ways that my body isn't accustomed to, but in ways that will benefit me.* Expect a little resistance when you begin to exercise some strategy, discipline, and perseverance. And expect to feel exhausted in the process. If you want to get to where you need to be, these three qualities are a must, so embrace it, accept it, roll up your sleeves, and get ready to get dirty!

After I left Brian, my *strategy* for getting dirty was to get back into school. Brian and I had been playing the breakup/makeup game for just over a year, and I knew that in order to stay focused, I needed to literally get away from him. I knew that I had to move to a different city and give myself a fresh start. So I moved with our ten-month old son to a small college town that was 200 miles away from home and immediately began to take classes at the local community college. It felt liberating, but this was no easy endeavor.

I exercised *discipline* when I had to manage my own finances for the first time. The last thing I wanted was to return home broke, homeless, and without a degree. I was extremely disciplined when it came to my studies. I took nothing for granted. Each time I set foot on campus or spent an entire night studying in the library (with my son in tow), I was thoroughly ecstatic to be a college student doing my thing. The gratefulness never wore out. It's part of what kept me going.

Perseverance was a constant for me as a twenty-year-old college student. The challenges seemed to arise at every turn. Between the rejection letters I received from the admissions office the first few times I applied to the university, losing child care for my son on three separate occasions, and running out of money half-way through the month, I had many opportunities to throw my hands up and accept the defeat I felt. But I was too hard-headed for that. I hung in there and persevered. I got to know the people in the admissions office. I took my son to class with me when I needed to. At one point, I even worked three jobs (including pizza delivery), just to make ends meet by the end of the month. I refused to be defeated and kept pushing forward until they handed me that diploma—a great reward for never bending, staying focused, and never losing faith.

In order to stay focused on moving forward, begin by deciding where you want to be. It's impossible to get to where you're going if you don't know your destination. Let's say you want to find yourself in a happy and fulfilling relationship. In order to get to that place, it's important that you get yourself on the right track. If you're still bitter and hurt about your previous relationship, you won't be able to carry your weight when you do find something that has healthy and fulfilling potential. If you don't believe that a happy and fulfilling relationship is even possible, you'll see no need to wholeheartedly do what it takes to develop such a relationship with someone.

All of this goal setting is not just about distracting yourself to get over a broken heart. You're getting yourself prepared for the next phase of your life. The longer you take to do that, the longer you will remain sitting exactly where you are right now. Picture the place you want to be in your life. Describe it. Write about it. Create a dream board to serve as a visual reminder. Then put all of your energy into getting there. When going through a difficult and depressing time, the worst thing you can do is focus on how difficult and depressing it all is. Instead, let your dream life be the carrot stick that keeps you moving forward. This is only the beginning. I never stopped after earning my degree. Once I got that taste of sweet success, I had to keep going forward for more!

Finding the Motivation

I'll let you in on how I get through even the smallest challenges in life, using running on the treadmill as an example. On days when I really don't want to work out, I fool myself into going to the gym by setting small goals each step of the way. From getting myself out of the car to finishing up the last minute of the workout, I play games with myself. There are many days when I pull up to the gym and I don't even want to get out of the car, when I'm tempted to go back home and curl up under my covers. On those days, I convince myself to just get on the treadmill and walk. That way, I can burn *some* calories and not feel like a total loser.

So I get out of my car. Once I get to the treadmill and I've done a five-minute warm-up walk, I tell myself that at the very least, I could run for one minute. *What's one minute?* So, I do it. After that minute, I challenge myself to increase the speed, and then to run for longer time frames. Or I'll run for ten-calorie intervals. Sometimes, I run until I reach a certain distance. Basically, I play little games with myself until the workout is complete. What happens is that once my body has experienced one victory, it actually wants more. And every time, I end up doing much more than I ever intended to do. I don't allow myself to become overwhelmed by the big picture. I stay focused on the smaller goal (running for sixty seconds) to get the larger goal accomplished (getting my workout in for the day).

Translate this strategy into accomplishing your own life goals when motivation is on empty—not by feeling overwhelmed by the ultimate goal, but by focusing on each of the smaller goals along the way, by playing games with yourself to get the small things done. And don't forget to celebrate each small victory as you go. These victories are a big deal! They are what make your ultimate dream possible.

Let's revisit that dream of enjoying a fulfilling, loving relationship. What type of woman do you think you'll need to be in order to have that relationship? What qualities will you need to have? What should your temperament be like? Those are the qualities you should be focused on developing. Don't obsess over finding a new relationship to replace the old one. Focus on preparing yourself for what it is you want. Because, really, what good is it to find that great guy and you're still a mess? Been there, done that. Not fun.

Now, let's say that you want to start your own business. The same questions apply. What type of woman will you need to be? What qualities would be essential? How should your temperament be? Once you've answered those questions, set smaller goals that will help you develop the qualities you'll need to successfully run your own business. Don't jump into starting the business without working on developing those core qualities. As you think about what those core qualities should be, keep that ultimate goal in mind. Never lose sight of that.

Keep your goals realistic. As you determine what you'll spend the next year developing professionally, set practical goals that you are capable of accomplishing within a reasonable timeframe. If you are currently a sales clerk and you want to be a lawyer, make it a goal to start taking classes this time next year, studying pre-law. In the meantime, spend this year doing what it will take for you to be enrolled in school no later than a year from now. Whatever you'd like to do professionally, getting there means being *strategic* (have a plan), *disciplined* (focused on the plan), and *persevering* (undeterred by challenges that come along the way).

The challenges will come. You may be tempted to go off course, but just because you experience those difficult, debilitating days from time to time does not mean that you get a pass to sit on your hands with your head hung low. If you expect to get beyond where you are today, do what it takes to make that happen. Strategy. Discipline. Perseverance. No ifs, ands, or buts about it. It's all up to you, girlfriend.

Love you,

Dr. Pamela

♥ INSPIRE YOUR HEART

1. My ideal life in one year looks like this:

2. What I would love to accomplish professionally:

3. Over the next year, I will do this to get myself at least one step closer to that accomplishment:

Letter 15

YOUR SPIRITUAL GOAL

My Sister,

I woke up this morning feeling compelled to write to you about finding peace. I know that in the midst of this emotional transition, there are times when you feel that you'll never come to a place of peace. You may even have a difficult time *picturing* peace in your life. I felt this way after Najee. I had totally built my world up around him. My present and my future simply didn't exist apart from him. But when it ended, I needed to find a way to exist without him. I needed to see above the debris that surrounded me so that I could realize that there was an even greater destiny for my life. If I could rise above the debris, I would see that I was on one small pit stop of the grand journey—a pit stop that was necessary to prepare and fine-tune me for what was ahead. Without that pit stop, I would not have been able to develop into the woman I am today and the woman I will become tomorrow.

Likewise, my sister, you will not be able to develop into the woman that you are destined to become without trudging through your own pit stops. Of course, you can't literally and physically rise above today's situation to see what's ahead and how this is all a part of getting you there, but your spiritual self *does* have the power to do that. Your body may be stuck in the mud and the debris of your circumstances, but our spirituality enables us to rise above it all to find peace and understanding. Spiritually, we can find peace and clarity through life's most challenging situations. If spirituality is not your thing, just hear me out before checking out.

What I found was that the only way I could truly let go was by finding peace with the situation and accepting it for what it was. I could do all of the refocusing I wanted but refocusing without truly finding peace with what I was going through would have been living in denial—pretending that everything was okay when it was not. That is definitely not what I'm encouraging you to do. I'm encouraging you to come to a place of true and total peace with where you are in life, and this comes from an understanding of where you are headed. One very important way of finding peace with where you are headed is through the understanding you gain spiritually.

It's our spiritual understanding that allows us to see the greater purpose in all things. This level of understanding allows us to rest assured that all things happen for a reason. Think about some of the most courageous women we know in history—St. Joan of Arc, Harriet Tubman, Coretta Scott King, Sojourner Truth, Helen Keller. These women endured incredibly trying times, but they weren't fixated on the impossible. They each focused on the bigger picture, the greater purpose in all things, on what was possible. This is where these women found strength. It takes a great amount of faith and spiritual discipline to maintain this type of focus. Each of these women were well developed spiritually, and it was this level of spirituality that enabled them to live with internal peace, despite the circumstances.

There's no question that Mrs. King had moments of fear and frustration as her family came under attack at every angle, yet she continued in the fight for civil rights, even after the death of her husband—until the day of her very own passing. Helen Keller was also relentless. Not only did she learn to read and write, but this woman—permanently blind and deaf from early childhood—became an advocate for human rights and wrote twelve books. Even in her physical blindness, she saw the bigger picture. Without a doubt, she had difficult days, but those days did not dominate or define her. She found greater purpose in her circumstance.

This level of spiritual maturity and strength doesn't happen overnight, of course. As with anything else, it takes time to grow and develop into maturity. It's one of those noble pursuits in life that we can never fully master. Spiritual maturity is a virtue to be gradually perfected each day over the course of our entire lives.

This last goal should be focused on developing your spiritual maturity and strength. Your spiritual self will help put things into perspective, and ultimately, will help you find peace. No matter where you are spiritually—whether you are totally disconnected or if you spend a great deal of time in prayer and meditation daily—there is always room for improvement. Do you feel a greater sense of purpose in your life, or do you feel totally lost in the world? Regardless of where you are on that continuum, building up your spiritual maturity and strength will give teeth to the other goals that you've set to this point. All other actions are pointless if you move forward without understanding that where you are today fits into the grand scheme of things.

Think about where you are spiritually. Where are you strengths and weaknesses? Do you have a network or even just *one* person who will support you spiritually? Who will impart words of wisdom that give you perspective and keep you grounded? Do you pray regularly? Do you meditate? Do you read spiritual material? Are you a part of a spiritual community? Do you attend services regularly? What goals can you set that will help you strengthen your spiritual life? There are a number of ways to develop yourself spiritually. I chose to do my spiritual work through my walk as a non-denominational Christian. You may have another preference. My intent here is not to promote a specific religion, activity, or ritual, but rather to pass along the very idea of strengthening your spirituality so that you may find greater understanding, and ultimately peace, with where you are today.

After the end of each of my relationships, I drew most of my strength through my consistent heart-felt conversations with God. When I left Brian, I spent a great deal of time developing my faith. Because I was taking a step into the unknown as a young, single mom, I concentrated on trusting God to guide me into the right direction and to provide my son and me with all of our basic needs. This was when I taught myself how to cover my fears with *faith* so that I could keep moving forward in the face of hopelessness.

But it was after leaving Jackson that I was most calculated about my spiritual growth, perhaps because going from wife to single mom of two was the most life-changing experience between the three breakups. After leaving Jackson, I immediately set three spiritual goals. I decided that I would find and join a women's bible study; that I would seek out a mentoring relationship with a strong woman of God who could fill my heart and spirit with wisdom; and that I would get ministerial training so that once this broken heart was healed, I could reach out to help someone else (you, perhaps?).

Now, of course, you don't have to set *three* spiritual goals, but I do encourage you to do what is necessary to strengthen yourself spiritually. Immersing myself into the development of my spiritual life was so therapeutic, I believe it was the one thing that was most effective in keeping me grounded. I allowed myself to cry when it hurt, to be uplifted by gospel music, to be encouraged by biblical scriptures, and to be enlightened by my pastor's sermons. Earlier I shared that after Jackson, I was going to church four times a week. This was primarily to avoid being miserable in my apartment. Sunday morning service, Monday night prayer, Wednesday night bible study, and Saturday night service. Crazy, right? It *was* a lot, but it kept me busy, and the routine rescued me from staying stuck in a rut for too long. And those ruts definitely do come, don't they?

The most tremendously helpful thing that I did was to develop a relationship with my pastor, Melva Henderson, an experienced no-nonsense woman of God who mentored me spiritually. As I was going through this process of letting go, I had many moments of doubt and fear. *Did I make the right decision? What if I just sentenced myself to a lifetime of loneliness?* Pastor Melva helped to keep things in perspective and reminded me that I was doing exactly what I needed to do to get myself back on track. Yes, my goals and activities were very church-oriented. That's what worked for me. In my time of isolation, I yearned for community, fellowship, and support, so I did what I needed to do to fulfill those needs. Your journey and your needs may be very different. What you decide to do to fulfill those needs is entirely up to you!

When life begins to feel lonely, it's so easy to doubt yourself or to become fearful that things will never change for the better. Pastor Melva kept reminding me that as long as I continued to improve myself and move forward with my life, things would *have* to change, and that I would never see the change if I became complacent. So I kept at it, and sure enough, change came—*divine* change that I could never have predicted for myself. It was change that I was unable to even imagine during those extremely hopeless moments of loneliness and fear. Pastor Melva poured so much wisdom and common sense and love and encouragement into me that I was well equipped with the strength and guidance I needed to weather the difficult times.

My outlook on life became more hopeful, my friendships more meaningful, and my challenges actually began to resolve themselves and work together in my favor. Not long after my divorce, when I could have been overwhelmed with worry over a salary that was not nearly enough to cover my bills, I stayed grounded in my faith and kept my eyes on the bigger picture. I knew that I was headed in the right direction in life and took comfort in knowing that if I kept pressing forward, I would soon be on an upswing.

And I was right. The evidence showed itself just one month after the divorce was final. After finding only *one* open faculty position in the entire state of Georgia that matched my qualifications and interests, I applied for the job. And guess what? Despite a shaky economy and record-high unemployment rates, I was offered *that* job with a salary that doubled what I was making before! And against *all* odds, even in the midst of the anger he felt toward me, and after threatening to take custody of our daughter, Jackson agreed to transfer his job to Georgia so that our daughter (the innocent bystander in all of this) could still have both of her parents nearby.

It was through all of these efforts to build up my spiritual life that I found peace. I was able to rest assured that this time of instability and fear was not all in vain. I had an *awesome* future ahead of me. I found peace in knowing that the mistakes I had made were gone. Peace in knowing I was living the best kind of life possible. I knew that what I was going through was temporary and that God was still looking out for me, even after all that I had gone through. Without this peace, there's no telling what I would have done out of desperation to make the hurt, the loneliness, and the fear go away. Some women fill that space with other men, others fill it with hate, mistrust, and bitterness, and others destroy their own bodies with risky behaviors. All of these choices can take us even further away from finding that better life. None of them result in real peace.

The only way to overcome the fear, doubt, and loneliness that can torment us after a relationship ends is by finding peace. *Real* peace. This peace enabled me to rise above the situation and live *beyond* what was going on in my little world. By rising above, I was able to see what was in the distance, and that perspective changed my behavior. I could map out a course for myself by listening to what God had been patiently trying to tell me all along: *Slow down. Stop trying to rush everything.* I found clarity by staying connected with my church and seeking the support of my pastor. Some may choose to go on a spiritual retreat. Others may prefer to immerse themselves in a period of fasting and prayer. There are endless options. I challenge you to take the time to figure out what it will take to build up your spiritual strength and maturity. I challenge you to find the greater purpose in all that you are going through right now so that you may find peace.

What has your spirit been trying to tell you? What do you need to do in order to hear this message clearly? What will you do to find peace? I strongly encourage you to get spiritually connected.

Love you lots,

Dr. Pamela

♥   **INSPIRE YOUR HEART**

1. What do I know I should be doing, but haven't yet begun to do?

2. What's holding me back?

3. What goals will I set that can help strengthen my spiritual life?

4. Who can I connect with to help me on this journey?

Letter 16

MY FINAL WORD ON REFOCUSING

My Sister,

Let's recap the concept of refocusing your goals. In order to help yourself move on and let go after a broken heart, it's essential that you take some time to practice goal setting. I strongly suggest that you set some goals for yourself in these four different categories:

Self-Improvement – What weakness do you have that you want to improve?
Strength – What are you good at doing that could be further developed?
Professional – What can you do to enhance your career?
Spiritual – What will help you see the greater purpose in your situation?

Do what works for you and make sure it's manageable—that you set goals you can realistically accomplish over the next year. Some goals may have a one-month deadline, others may be six-month goals, and another could be accomplished a year from now. Whatever you do, make them practical and realistic enough to reached. The idea is that you build yourself up by watching yourself blossom, rather than tearing yourself down by setting goals that are unreasonably complicated. It's time to make it happen. Pull out your computer, a notepad, or the notes application on your cell phone—whatever is most practical for you. Jot down at least one goal you'll accomplish from each category: self-improvement, strength, professional, and spiritual. After you've identified a goal for each, print them out and keep them in a place that is easily accessible as a reminder of what you should be working on.

Get Some Accountability Partners

And that's not all! Find someone who will hold you accountable—someone that you trust—and send your goals to them. When I wrote up my goals after leaving Jackson, I emailed them off to two of my life processors—girlfriends who were very supportive of me. They loved my goals and periodically checked in to see if I was making any progress. They kept me encouraged and were thrilled right along with me as I accomplished each one.

This is no time to be too proud to reach out for help. You need people, and it's important that you are willing to open up so that you can get the support you need and deserve. If you don't have it, go find it! You've got to do what you must to get what you need.

If you can recall from one of my earlier letters, I pointed out that refocusing means to find a new central point of interest, to change what you give your attention to and the activities in which you chose to partake. My strategy for refocusing after each of my relationships ended was to embrace those people in my life who were positive influences and who had my best interests at heart, to rearrange my routine and priorities, and to identify and work toward a new set of goals. Through this effort to refocus, I was able to keep myself moving forward and out of

Woe-is-me-ville. I was able to position myself to receive greater opportunities by choosing not to spend time dwelling on what was gone while worrying about the future. I was focused on my climb.

The key is that I didn't just stay busy for the purpose of detaching myself from what was happening in my life. The fact is I was going through a major life transition, so in all of my busyness and goal setting, I made it a point to *address* the transition by taking care of my emotional health and by staying in contact with key people who could help me process it all. Between the professional therapist, my spiritual mentors, and a few friends who were great at listening and asking questions, I was well supported.

I knew I needed an entourage. Be real with yourself about what you need to do to refocus. This is the first key to letting go, moving forward, and healing after a broken heart. Do everything in your power not to dwell on the pain, the emptiness, or the disappointments. Focus on what you do have and what you can become.

The next key to letting go requires that you dig in and do some internal repair work. This is *rebuilding*. In my next set of letters, I'll tell you how I went about rebuilding myself from the inside out. I needed to be more than just a shell of a person. Sure, I was professionally successful, I had a great set of people in my corner, and I was in the best physical shape of my life (exercise is a great stress reliever), but I needed to be whole and healthy on the inside, too. Many people do the refocusing part really well, and then they stop there. They go into the next phase of their lives an empty shell—still hurt, still resentful, and driven by a fear of being hurt again. I don't want this to happen to you. So, now that we've covered the easy part—refocusing—

let's roll up our sleeves and go for the gusto. Now, my sister, let's look more closely at you. Let's rebuild you.

Love,

Dr. Pamela

THE ART OF
REBUILDING

CHAPTER FIVE

REBUILD YOUR SELF-ESTEEM

In my eyes EVERYTHING is beautiful. I even hurt sometimes and see the beauty in that. I am reminded of my own humanity and my continuing journey to healing. Each time I discover a new issue, wound, scar, habit, response or condition in myself, I am excited. Because it means I have found the next thing to address and improve and wash clean. And I can keep getting better at being me.

- Saddi Khali, photographer, philosopher, social critic
Facebook Post, December 18, 2012

Letter 17

PICKING UP THE PIECES

My Sister,

All right, my friend, it's time to rebuild! After coming out of a relationship, even if it wasn't totally devastating, we tend to carry along some of the wounds from the process. These wounds affect how we view relationships. Sometimes, these wounds can cause us to throw up our defenses to avoid more pain, or to run rather than taking the time to heal.

A brief bout with bitterness after heartbreak is natural. Our defense mechanisms step in to ensure that we don't get hurt again. But this is a knee-jerk reaction. After having some time to sit down and think, it is essential to come away from the knee-jerk mentality and settle into a more calculated, reasonable one. That is, if we ever want to move forward and enjoy a healthy, loving relationship in the future.

We experience such pain when a relationship ends because when someone who was a huge part of our lives leaves, the splitting up is just that—a splitting. Splitting apart what used to be a shared life into two separate lives. This is not always a neat and easy split. The process can get quite messy. When I was going through my divorce, I often heard that a marriage ending is like a ripping—it can be painful, stressful, messy, and traumatizing. I will venture to say that this also applies to long-term, intimate relationships. When something is ripped apart, it's not a neat process.

Imagine breaking a stick of taffy in half by pulling it apart. First of all, this doesn't happen very easily. It takes quite a bit of tugging, twisting, and turning. The same occurs within the context of a struggling relationship. Couples often experience some painful tugging before the split actually happens. Both parties are stretched thin, perhaps with one wanting to go and the other wanting to stay, but both exhausted from the wear and tear of stretching, fighting, crying, trying, and failing. Yet, after enough of that pulling and stretching, the break finally happens. And what does taffy look like once it's been pulled apart? It looks distressed! The ends that endured the break are jagged and thinned out from being pulled. These thinned out, jagged edges indicate that the split was not a clean one, that parts of you went with him and parts of him stayed with you. That taffy, if it ever wants to be marketable again, needs to be rebuilt.

You need to be rebuilt. Regardless of whether or not you initiated or caused the split, a major piece of your life, your being, and your identity has been left with thinned out, jagged edges. Repackaging the damaged end with a stunning new career and a sexy new wardrobe sells yourself short. It is only a matter of time before everyone sees right through your façade, which eventually will become just as obvious as the disguise of a crackhead who has thrown on some lipstick and a wig to cover it all up. Remember the crackhead? You may be slick enough to pull it off at first, but if you keep ignoring the problem, your issues will eventually show themselves to the world whether you like it or not—in your work performance, in your attitude, even in your appearance and demeanor.

Rebuild yourself. You've got a whole future of opportunities ahead of you, and you want to be sure that you are ready and whole when they come knocking.

What it Means to Rebuild

When you rebuild, essentially what you are doing is repairing the damage. Most dictionary definitions describe rebuilding as dismantling and reassembling with new parts. It's a process that can include *replacing, restrengthening, revising,* or *reorganizing.* We often associate rebuilding with what is done after a natural disaster of sorts—a hurricane, an earthquake, a tsunami. In the aftermath of a disaster, there is *much* to be repaired, from the buildings that may have toppled to the ground to each broken bone and shattered dream suffered. This repairing is done by dismantling damaged homes and reassembling them with new parts; by replacing broken pavement with fresh, new cement; by restrengthening weakened bridges so that they are stable once again. When you rebuild, you take something that has been damaged and distressed and make it new again.

I equate the breakdown of my marriage to a devastating flood. I always knew that the sands Jackson and I had built our relationship upon were unstable and that we needed to move to higher ground, but we never did. We just taped plastic to the windows and coated the exterior with pretty waterproof paint, hoping that a flood would never actually come. But guess what? The flood came. And when those floodwaters came sweeping in, *everything* was wiped away, leaving behind only a shell of a home. On the outside, no one could tell that the inside was hollowed out. Even that elegantly painted shell would only be able to hold itself up for so long without its internal foundation. After the flood, there was nothing left to go back to. All that was in me for Jackson and our marriage had died. My affinity for him was swept away with the flood, and I knew that everything I had held on to for so many years—the hopes that he would finally fall in love with me, the blind determination to make it work no matter what, the dream of happily ever after—had also been swept away.

Some of what did stick with me, however, desperately needed to be replaced—the low self-esteem, the reluctance to speak up for myself, the fear of being abandoned, credit problems, and a whole lot of resentment. This flood left me empty and in desperate need of repair. I didn't even realize until after I left Jackson that I had been living each day on edge, under pressure, and heavily burdened. It wasn't until I left and felt lighter and more alive than ever that I realized what this marriage had been doing to me. Though I experienced a great sense of relief, I had to repair parts of myself that I didn't even know were broken. It took some time and real diligence to discover where my wounds were and then to repair each of them one by one. Sounds exhausting, doesn't it? It is exhausting. But it's worth it to uncover your wounds and heal them so that they don't take you by surprise and weigh you down later.

Everyone's experiences are different and result in different types of damages. Some of us come out of hurricanes, while others survive earthquakes, snowstorms, or cougar attacks. What was your disaster? What do you need to rebuild as a result? In my next set of letters to you, I'll focus on three particular facets of rebuilding: your self-esteem, your strength, and your ability to trust.

There is a calm and a peace that comes after the storm, and though at times it may seem that the calmness is much too quiet or lonely for your taste, take full advantage of it. There is no time like the present—after the storm has passed—to get on your feet and start rebuilding so that you'll be stronger, more confident, and more positive than ever before.

Love You,

Dr. Pamela

Letter 18

KNOWING YOUR WORTH

My Sister,

    Growing up, I was fortunate enough to have parents who constantly encouraged me, lifted me up, and told me how great I was. I thank God for that, because this planted a deeply rooted seed with the belief that I deserved to be treated a certain way. I had a small understanding of my worth, which was enough to compel me to walk away from Brian without looking back. It took me a little longer with Jackson, but I always knew when I was with him that I could be treated better. I was worth more than he was giving, yet in spite of what I knew, I still doubted myself.

    When I first left Jackson, I had many moments of questioning whether or not I had made the right decision, whether or not I had overreacted, if it was realistic for me to expect something different or to want more out of our marriage. That's when an amazing woman (a voice of experience) stepped into my life and shared three words with me that I will never forget: KNOW YOUR WORTH. With those three words, she managed to fertilize that little seed that my parents had planted many years ago. *I am a woman of great worth.* At the age of thirty-three, I was reminded of this powerful truth—a truth that I hadn't heard in at least a decade.

Linda was a woman of power and confidence who had solidly understood her worth for many years. She chose a loving and devoted husband who thoroughly understood her worth. It was inspiring to be in the presence of those two during a time when it was easy to dismiss true love as something that only existed in fairy tales. Linda was a voice of experience, not as a result of overcoming a failed marriage, but because she had experienced heartbreak as a child and understood the important shielding power of knowing her worth.

Know your worth. The moment she spoke those words to me, they resonated like a rush of clarity, bursting through my veins, speaking to my very soul, clearing out all questions, doubts, and insecurities. That was it! That was precisely what I had lost sight of at some point in my marriage and in all of my relationships. I had forgotten my worth. I had forgotten that knowing my worth even mattered. I was worth so much more than what I had settled for over the years. I was a far cry from the young woman who, almost a decade before, had purchased her own home, had built up her credit, and as a single mom, had graduated with a master's degree—all by age twenty-six. Somewhere between then and my decision to walk down the aisle, I had forgotten my worth. So worried about being a single mom for the rest of my life, I had locked my worth in a closet and handed the key over to someone who also did not understand my worth.

I had forgotten—until the day I sat before Linda and poured my heart out to her about how I had managed to fool everyone into thinking I was happy and that our family was stable. The time had come to face my reality. I didn't know how to come to terms with all of it. *How do I know if I'm doing the right thing?* And the answer to all of my questions was wisely rolled up into three simple words: KNOW YOUR WORTH.

From this point on, my sister, I want you to reclaim an understanding of your worth. If you've never known your worth before, now is the perfect time to get acquainted. First and foremost, understand and accept that you are worthy of being loved, valued, and respected. If at the very least, you have not yet come to accept this as truth, then you certainly have not yet acknowledged your worth. Before you can expect anyone to love, value, and respect you, you've got to love, value, and respect yourself! In all that you do, you're showing people how you expect to be treated. If you don't know how to treat yourself, well, there's not a whole lot of promise that you'll be able to teach others how to love, value, and respect you. "Others" can be your friends, colleagues, family members, or a new significant other. It doesn't matter who it is. You should require that all people you interact with know your worth. But *you* have to know it first.

One of the ways to do this is to take some of the refocusing strategies from the first three chapters very seriously. By focusing on goals that encourage you to develop your strengths, and by surrounding yourself with people who uplift and encourage you, you'll effectively boost your sense of self. In other words, start immersing yourself in the positive. This is not the time to be surrounded with negativity. Flee from anything negative. If negativity takes hold of you, there goes your sense of self and all of your progress toward letting go and moving forward. Do everything in your power to stay positive. Remind yourself of your strengths. If ever you forget your worth, call up an uplifter or a voice of experience and tell them what you're feeling. If you have good, effective people in your corner, it won't take long for them to bring you back to your senses.

Learning to Help Myself

Without a doubt, having positive people around to bring you out of your rut is a great thing, but there comes a point when you have to be able to do this for yourself. For one thing, your entourage of heart healers do have their own concerns— boyfriends, wives, children, jobs, interests. You can't reasonably expect to be the center of their lives. They won't always be able to drop everything and run to your rescue when you're having "a moment."

I'll admit it. Those were some of the toughest times for me— when I was having a woe-is-me moment and my heart healers were nowhere to be found. There were times when I would go almost a week without hearing my phone ring. It was as if the whole world was going about its business, and every last person on the planet had forgotten that I was right there, still living and breathing, but living and breathing *alone*. I hated those days. In those rare moments, I hated men collectively for rejecting me. I envied people who seemed to have amazing lives, and I was flat-out irritated with mushy gushy couples in love. I was not always a bright ray of sunshine, so I wouldn't be surprised if I became a drain even to my trusty uplifters.

For whatever reason, there were times when I found myself alone, and during those times, I had to deliberately pull myself out of my own rut. I refused to allow myself to sink too deeply into Woe-is-me-ville. My strategy was threefold. I talked to myself, I talked to God, and I lived stress-free. Each of these tactics helped me to remember my worth and that I was smack dab in the middle of one of the most important transformations of my life.

Talking to Myself

I often had to verbally remind myself that the only way to come out on the other side was to hang in there and to keep walking forward. I spoke out loud about all that I was grateful for. I reminded myself of all that I had done well and the accomplishments I had achieved in my life. I told myself that being alone in that moment was not a tragedy but an opportunity. A *forced* opportunity to look at myself, to reflect, and to work on my game plan—not to waste by dragging myself through Woe-is-me-ville. I encouraged myself in the way that my uplifters and voices of experience would, and I challenged myself to stay the course the way my life processors would.

Having time to yourself (whether by choice or by design) gives you a great opportunity to test your independence. It's emotionally dangerous to become so dependent upon other people that you're unable to get over some of the hurdles alone. Without a doubt, having people who love and support you is important and beneficial, but in those moments when you're not feeling the love and support, it has to be up to you to provide that for yourself. This reminds me of the words to the song *Encourage Yourself* by Donald Lawrence and the Tri-City Singers. Encourage yourself. Speak victory through the test.

I did a whole lot of encouraging myself in my low moments— a whole lot of speaking out loud when it was just me, myself, and I. It's absolutely essential that you come to a point where your own encouragement and your own understanding of your worth is sufficient to pull yourself out of a rut. This is important because the ultimate goal is that you come out of this transition with the ability to stand on your own two feet.

Talking to God

When I talk to God during really difficult times, there's no dignified strategy. I just start talking. I often begin with pathetic begging. My thoughts are scattered. All I feel is emotion. Pain. Desperation. Fear. So, I cry out, speaking through tears—speaking whatever flows out of me. And this is okay! This pathetic begging is so absolutely real and straight from the heart that it can be powerfully effective. I have cried out with words like, *Please take this feeling away! I just want to be happy. Please. Let me be happy.* I talk to God about how I am feeling and ask for peace. I ask for guidance and clarity so that I can know how to get through these moments and the difficult phases of my life. And in the end, I always find myself thanking God for where I am headed, for keeping me, for watching over me, for getting me over this hump. My conversations with God calm me down quite a bit. I'm able to find that peace of mind I referred to when I wrote about strengthening the spiritual self in Letter 15.

Living Stress-Free

Living as stress-free as possible is extremely important to me. Understand this: stress is a part of life. We can't always avoid it. So when I say stress-free, I mean that we are not *bound* by stress. We are free in spite of it. Stressful situations occur, and we are not toppled over by them. We don't internalize them. We are proactive about taking stressful situations in stride and keeping the stress *out* of our bodies.

With a family history of ailments that are exasperated by stress, I took great measures to ensure that I would not let stress get the best of me. I reminded myself to look at the big picture. That reminder alone was enough to calm me down and help me find ways to relax. I was not about to allow a lonely weekend affect my long term health and livelihood. I engaged in stress-relieving activities, which sometimes included treating myself to a massage, but almost always included writing and exercising. When I sat down to write, I poured out exactly how I was feeling on paper. I wrote letters and poetry, and sometimes, I would just free write—let my pen express whatever came to mind. Writing was a way of releasing the thoughts and feelings that were locked deep inside of me. This also allowed me to be very real with myself. It was always refreshing not to have to wear a mask or hold back what was really on my mind and in my heart.

Exercising, another stress reliever, did the exact opposite. Instead of helping me connect to my inner thoughts and feelings, it allowed me to *escape* for about an hour or two. The best part was always after the workout, because not only was I on a high from the rush of endorphins, I felt great about myself for getting it done. I felt gorgeous and sexy because I knew that the sweat and the hard work were great for my body.

Whether encouraged and uplifted by friends or self-encouraged, these tactics effectively kept me aware of my worth. I understood, ultimately, that I deserved to be respected, loved, and valued, by whatever means necessary. If it meant going through periods of loneliness, knowing that the alternative was to settle for less than I was worth, I made it a point to barrel down and persevere. I am worth it. The reward is worth it.

You are worth it, my sister. No matter how difficult the trials, how long or lonely or frustrating the days, stick to your guns. Never settle for less than what you deserve. Know your worth.

Love,

Dr. Pamela

Letter 19

TAKING CONTROL

My Sister,

At this transitional point in your life, there may seem to be much that you don't have control over. You can't wave a magic wand and make the relationship what you wanted it to be. You can't undo any of the decisions you made in the past. And you can't propel yourself into the future before it is due to arrive. But you *can* work with where you are at this moment.

Focusing on all of the things that you can't control will do nothing to help your self-esteem. It will only make you feel more hopeless and less competent. Rather than worrying over things that are beyond your control, try becoming excellent at taking control of what you can, while managing those things that you cannot. By *managing*, I mean accept that the situation is what it is and choose to do the best you can to work around those circumstances that are out of your hands.

One important aspect of my life that suffered after the divorce was my financial stability, particularly my credit rating. Before I moved from California to the Midwest to marry Jackson, I owned my own home and had pretty good credit. I created and maintained a system for managing my finances that was infallible. When I moved, I sold my house and used the profit to make a down payment on our new house. I taught

Jackson my financial system and entrusted it to him while I focused on my studies. But by the time our marriage ended five years later, we were faced with foreclosure and a credit score that seemed to enjoy free-falling as a favorite pastime. I had no idea we were in such financial danger. This did not come to light until after I filed for divorce. Again, I wasn't paying attention.

Jackson hadn't paid our property taxes for two years, all the while assuring me that our taxes were taken care of. Because my name was the one that appeared first on the deed to our house, I was the one the state went after just before the divorce was final. It was *my* meager salary they threatened to garnish as Jackson sat back and let them have their way with my income. Unfortunately, there was very little I could do about this because any joint finances Jackson chose to neglect out of his anger also hurt me. I was unable to buy a house, and even renting an apartment was more of a challenge than I had expected.

In the meantime, Jackson's life seemed to go on without a care in the world. He was smart enough to know how to incur debt that would negatively affect me, while enabling himself to maintain a life that was more luxurious and more exciting than the life we had shared in the five years that we were married. It frustrated the heck out of me to hear that he was able to purchase a luxury car, refurnish his home with flashy new appliances, and take ski trips while I was using the bulk of my money to pay down debt that he was primarily responsible for incurring. In Jackson's view, I was justifiably reaping the consequences of leaving him. It didn't seem fair. I often found myself consumed with frustration and anger over the fact that there were no quick solutions to this enormous problem.

From my standpoint, the situation was hopelessly overwhelming. I was constantly at battle with myself to keep woe-is-me off my shoulders. My life processors all echoed the exact same message when I fell into a hopeless mindset: *take control over what you can control*. The rest will work itself out. The message was not a rosy feel-good one, but it made sense, and it was absolutely true. When I placed less emphasis on what I couldn't fix right away and more emphasis on what I could, I was able to reclaim some control and feel a bit more competent.

No, I couldn't instantly send my credit score back to where it was, but I *could* develop a strategy for how I would rebuild it by taking control of my finances and having my name removed from as many joint accounts as possible. The strategy I developed was not a quick fix, but it was an effective one. Though it took some time to get it together, I experienced a boost to my self-esteem each time I successfully paid off a bill and watched my credit score slowly rise. The alternative would have been a self-destructive one. I could have chosen to sulk or to allow my anger to take over. Rather than working towards a solution that I could execute on my own, I may have wasted more time arguing with my ex over why he did this, why he didn't do that, and blah, blah, blah. It just would not have been a productive way to use my energy. The result of my diligence and God's grace? Within one year of the divorce, I was able to purchase a much nicer home than the one Jackson and I had as a married couple. And because I had a stronger credit score, the interest rate was so low that my payments were lower than what I would've paid renting a three-bedroom apartment. *Take control of what you can control, and the rest will follow.*

Another way that I took control was by checking my attitude. When my relationships with both Brian and Jackson first ended, they each responded with anger by blaming and attempting to intimidate me. With Jackson, I made a decision very early on that the divorce process needed to be as cordial as possible for our daughter's sake. Although I couldn't control his actions, I made it a point to keep my own in check. In the end, this proved to minimize the drama and caused him to rethink his own attitude. Ultimately, Jackson was much more cooperative than he would have been had I decided to engage in an emotionally charged battle with him. The outcome was the same after Brian and I broke up. It took many years, but I watched him evolve from being utterly difficult and violently irrational to humble, respectful, and cooperative. I couldn't control Brian's and Jackson's actions or decisions, but I certainly could control my own, and by doing so, each situation only continued to improve for all of us.

Are you dwelling on challenges that you have no control over? Don't. There's nothing you can do directly to change a person, to change the past, or to rush the future. But you can take actions that have the power to influence how people respond to you. Actions that help to remedy past hurts and regrets. Actions that set you up for a promising future. Your actions, decisions, and mindset are three things you *do* have control over. The way you handle each of these will make all the difference in not only the outcomes, but also in how you feel about yourself. If you make wise decisions, keep your actions in check, and maintain a positive mindset, you will be excellent at controlling the things that you *can*. This is absolutely essential to keeping your self-esteem up. Take the control over your life out of the hands of others. Reclaim it.

To avoid sliding backwards and getting sucked into a web of anger and bitterness, look at your situation. Honestly determine what you can control and then take control. If you're facing challenges that seem to be beyond your control, cut those challenges up into bite-sized pieces and focus on those pieces that you can address on your own. Develop strategies for how you'll resolve those bite-sized pieces over time. Don't let your challenges consume you. Outsmart them with strategy, and watch your self-esteem rise as you conquer obstacle after obstacle. Ending the relationship may not have been your choice or your preference, but now that you are sitting in this predicament today, think about how you will take the reins to rebuild your self-esteem and enhance your situation. It's up to you to determine the direction for the next phase of your life. You're in control!

Love,

Dr. Pamela

♥ INSPIRE YOUR HEART

Things I Cannot Change	Things I Can Change

1. How will I manage those things I cannot change?

2. How will I take control of those things that I can change?

Serenity Prayer: God, grant me the serenity to accept the things I cannot change, the courage to change the things I can, and the wisdom to know the difference. Think about it.

Letter 20

BUILDING IMMUNITY

My Sister,

Your self-esteem is one of the most important internal elements to rebuild over the next year, because really, your self-esteem will absolutely make or break how successful you are at letting go and moving forward with your life. It lays the foundation for your strength. Everything you do in this next year has the potential to elevate how you feel about yourself in ways you didn't know were possible. It's important that you strategically do what is necessary to build your self-esteem.

Self-esteem is all about how you view yourself. It entails what you believe you can do, how fond you are of yourself, and how other people's views of you affect your view of yourself. When you have a strong sense of self, you view yourself from these perspectives positively. People who have a poor sense of self do not have much faith in what they are able to accomplish. They are not very fond of themselves. They internalize the negative opinions they believe others may have of them. This can be a pretty vulnerable time in your life. I strongly suggest taking the reins and making it an *empowering* time. By building up your self-esteem, you are ensuring that this process of letting go is liberating and empowering. This, my friend, will be what makes the most difference in your ability to move on and to move on quickly.

Oprah Winfrey once said something about self-esteem that I'll never forget. She was talking to a mother about how to protect her daughter from becoming dangerously vulnerable in a relationship. Simply put, her message to that mother was to recognize the power of self-esteem. She said that mothers who instill self-esteem in their daughters essentially *immunize* them from getting caught up in an abusive relationship. Powerful! And this powerful little nugget also applies to you. Think of your self-esteem as your immunity—your defense against people and relationships that can pull you down. It is absolutely essential that you rebuild that immunity, especially when you're in a vulnerable place. Just as you would take measures to build up your health and immunity when you catch a cold, it is important to do the same to build up your self-esteem after experiencing something as emotionally draining and devastating as heartbreak.

Think about some of the most fundamental things we do when we get sick. We generally take several precautions including taking medication, visiting a doctor, getting a lot of rest, and avoiding over-exertion. If we take these precautions, the body generally responds by picking it up from there to heal itself.

Treating a Cold		Treating Low Self-Esteem
Take Medication	→	Take in Positive Reinforcement
Visit a Doctor	→	Visit a Professional
Get a Lot of Rest	→	Get Some "Me Time"
Avoid Over-Exertion	→	Avoid Negative Energy

A similar method can apply to building up your self-esteem:

Take in positive reinforcement – Usher in as much encouragement and support as possible.

Visit a professional – See a life coach or therapist to help uncover and address insecurities, especially if positive reinforcement doesn't seem to be enough.

Get some "me time" – Take time to escape and do what you enjoy away from the busy seriousness of life that can wear us down.

Avoid negative energy – Don't engage in activities or situations that can make you feel worse about yourself.

Take in Positive Reinforcement

Taking in positive reinforcement is like taking medication. It supports the immune system by helping to fight off whatever is attacking the body. In the same way, positive reinforcement supports the self-esteem by helping to fight off negative messages and experiences that can attack us from day to day. Positive reinforcement strengthens a weakened self-esteem. Like medicine, positive reinforcement is available in many forms. It can come through supportive friends (or your heart healers), the words you speak to yourself, or activities that make you feel great about yourself. All forms of positive reinforcement help to combat negative feelings and beliefs that can weaken and break down the self-esteem.

For starters, it's absolutely essential that you are careful about the words you speak to yourself. This is not the time to call yourself stupid, lazy, pitiful, pathetic, or whatever other negative words you may be tempted to speak. This is a time when you have to be intentional about speaking positively about yourself. *I am awesome. I rocked in that meeting today. My life is on an upswing. I am on the verge of greatness.* Don't wait for other people to tell you these things, say them to yourself. Work them into your conversations. It won't be long before the people who love and respect you begin to echo these affirmations for you.

Positive reinforcement can also be accomplished through your actions. When I felt down on myself, my outlet was to create something. I would create through writing, making jewelry, cooking, or even graphically designing something on the computer. This always proved to be a great means of positively reinforcing my strengths. It felt freeing to spend time writing a new poem or concocting a new recipe, because when I was done expending my energy on something I loved to do, I had the reward of reveling in my new creation. I took great pride in reading my new masterpiece aloud or indulging in a new dish that I swore would be a hit on The Food Network. This was a really easy way of reminding myself of my strengths without having to rely on others to do that for me.

Visit a Professional

Sometimes the negative feelings and beliefs we have of ourselves are so deeply engrained that positive reinforcement is simply not enough to bring us out of a negative mindset and strengthen the self-esteem. We may not know where our insecurities come from or that we even *have* them until we are surprised by them one day. That is exactly what happened to me. When I began dating after ending the marriage with Jackson, I was totally caught off guard by an insecurity that I didn't realize I had.

I had always considered myself an affectionate person, but Jackson rarely showed me any affection. I yearned for him to hold my hand, play with my hair, kiss me randomly—to just make *any* romantic, affectionate gesture—but he would not. When I motioned for affection by reaching for his hand, he'd pull away and say it wasn't his style. This always confused me, because I often had the pleasure of witnessing the extreme (almost exaggerated) level of affection he gave to the other women in his family. He never really let those walls down for me. That hurt for a long time, but after awhile, I got so used to the rejection and lack of affection, I just accepted this as a part of our reality. Being rejected wasn't fun, so I inadvertently built up a wall of defense of my own and carried it into my next dating situation with Najee.

To my complete shock, Najee commented one day on how un-affectionate I was. *What? Me?!* He said that I was so closed up that he didn't feel I would be receptive to any affectionate gesture he might make. I was totally shocked by this because everything inside of me still *craved* affection. I didn't realize until he said it that the affectionate side of me had walls built all around it. I couldn't deny how completely right he was. Even after I was aware of this and made a conscious decision to open up, I found it especially difficult to initiate affection—to do something even as simple as grab his hand or spontaneously throw my arms around him. I *so* wanted to, but I couldn't bring myself to do it because I was terrified that he would reject me. Not long after that revelation, I decided to see a therapist again to address issues like these—baggage from past relationships that I didn't know was there—to minimize the likelihood that another one of my skeletons would creep up on me out of the blue. Amazingly, my therapist and I were able to uncover a number of hidden insecurities that I had been carrying, all of which greatly affected my interactions with others. Clearly, my positive reinforcements weren't quite enough to resolve those deeply rooted fears. I needed to talk it through with an expert.

Get Some "Me Time"

Our lives can get pretty exhausting at times. Mentally, emotionally, and physically draining. Being busy is a good thing. It can keep our minds from becoming idle and depressed. But *exhaustion* can do a number on self-esteem, especially when we're struggling to stay on top of everything. Even after a breakup, life continues on. It's up to us to keep moving right along with it. We've got jobs, kids, bills to pay, projects to complete, and other relationships to maintain. We don't all get to jump on a plane and spend a year touring Italy, India, and Indonesia to find ourselves after a breakup. But if you can make that happen, do it!

For the rest of us, when working on rebuilding self-esteem, it is essential to take a break from the hustle and bustle and find ways to stop, relax, and take care of ourselves. I'm notorious for building me time right into my work schedule. I'll grab a Tuesday and smack a two-hour block of time on my calendar and call it "meeting" so I could go get a massage, have a long lunch at a nice restaurant, go somewhere to exercise, or sneak in a nap (I actually keep a sleeping bag in my office). Whatever it is that I need, I'll go do it. My friends get a kick out of this and think I'm nuts, but they all say that they wish they could do the same. I tell them that they can if it's important enough. "Me time" is just as important as (if not more) than any other meeting on my calendar. Taking time away from the craziness of life allows you those needed moments of peace and a chance to treat yourself the way you desire to be treated. You set the example for others. If you don't pamper yourself from time to time (or heck, all of the time), how will anyone else know that this is important to you?

Steal some time away for yourself. Stay physically and mentally healthy, and you'll begin to experience the strengthening of your self-esteem. You'll love yourself for it. And as others begin to see your pattern of self-care, they too will begin to reinforce your positive sense of self. It really does begin with you.

Avoid Negative Energy

When you're working on building self-esteem, make sure you are as progressive as possible. Continue to advance and move forward in life rather than slide backwards. Engaging in activities that don't honor your strengths and primarily highlight your weaknesses can stifle your progress. Simply put, try to spend less time on the things that you suck horribly at, and spend more time doing what makes you feel competent, strong, beautiful, and energized.

I assume that you'd never go mountain climbing in the snow while fighting the flu, because that certainly wouldn't build up your immune system. It would make you feel worse. The same applies to building up your self-esteem. This is not the time to pursue projects or initiatives that bring more stress and frustration than peace and satisfaction. If at all possible, avoid activities or situations that bring you down until your self-esteem is stronger. Of course, this is easier said than done, as these tasks can't always be avoided, especially if they are a part of how you make a living. If you can't avoid doing the grunt work, do the best you can to go heavy on the feel-good stuff while keeping the feel-bad stuff to a minimum. Rebuilding your self-esteem should be a priority. Do whatever you can to protect and support it.

Just as it is important to avoid activities that are draining and highlight your weaknesses, it's also important to avoid activities that compromise your dignity. For many of us, going through a breakup can be a very vulnerable and unstable time. Some people respond with anger and are tempted to take revenge by engaging in behaviors such as destroying property or using the kids against the ex. I've seen situations in which men and women alike become *consumed* with jealousy and expend a great deal of energy investigating what the ex is doing, who the ex is seeing, and in some cases, attempt to sabotage the ex's future relationships. Some people even turn on themselves and become involved in self-destructive behaviors such as sexual carelessness or excessive substance abuse.

All such responses to a breakup, no matter how liberating or justified they may feel at the moment, compromise your dignity. This only causes more harm to your self-esteem because if you're on the road to living a more empowered and productive life, you'll eventually feel like crap—like you slid backwards big time—for causing a scene or becoming obsessed over finding the new person in their life. Your dignity comes from knowing that you are the bigger person, that you are growing each day (rather than regressing), that you are stronger than the voice that tempts you to do something that is just flat-out stupid. It's simply not worth risking your self-esteem over. Hold on to your dignity with both hands and both feet if you have to. Do nothing—nothing at all—to compromise it.

Your self-esteem is priceless. It is the single most important aspect of yourself that makes letting go and moving forward possible. A strong self-esteem will make you *beautiful* enough to attract someone who sees your beauty, *intelligent* enough to create an amazing life for yourself, *secure* enough to enjoy that life to its fullest, *strong* enough to thrive during difficult times, and *irresistible* enough to surround yourself with equally irresistible people. When you believe in yourself and feel good about yourself, your whole world view changes, and in turn, your whole world changes.

I don't want to oversimplify this. Let's be clear that rebuilding self-esteem is not easy, especially if you are building from scratch. It takes deliberate effort. You have to build it up *intentionally.* This means being aware and executing a plan, day by day, minute by minute, thought by thought. It means checking yourself if you are tempted to engage in an undignified, stupid act. It means going out of your way to have fun and spoil yourself. It means staying away from people who bring you down and spending lots of time with people who make you feel great about yourself.

When I was rebuilding my self-esteem after my divorce, many people commented that they saw a physical change in me. I was changing from the inside out. Because I felt so good about myself for the first time in many years, I began to take better care of myself. I exercised, I ate better, I laughed more. My skin became more radiant, I dropped four jean sizes, and my hair looked healthier and stronger than ever before. People often told me that I had a glow that they had never seen. I began to truly love myself and my new life because I was strengthening my self-esteem on purpose. I clung to people who didn't hesitate to compliment me, and I refused to interact with negative people who tried to bring me down. I wrote letters to myself and took self-portraits with my camera phone on my "good days." I would do whatever it took to convince myself that I was beautiful, intelligent, strong, and irresistible.

This is not about arrogance or conceit. The idea is to build up your self-esteem so that you can live out your life purpose and be a positive influence in the lives of others. Be proactive about it. Because until *you* get on board, there is absolutely nothing that anyone outside of you can do to build you up. If you take medication for a fever and your immune system refuses to get on board, that medication is totally useless. In the same sense, you could be the finest chick in the room, getting compliments left and right. You could have friends who wish they were as funny or intelligent or professional as you are. You could have the greatest life coach ever. But if *you* are not on board—if *you* are not proactive about rebuilding your own self-esteem—none of those outside forces will matter.

Whether you have a lot of rebuilding to do or just a little, make it a point to pay attention and take action. Otherwise, you risk allowing the self-esteem you *do* have to weaken, and that will affect your ability to let go. Make it happen. Build yourself up, so that you can let go and move forward.

Peace,

Dr. Pamela

♥ INSPIRE YOUR HEART

1. How is my self-esteem? If I had to rate myself on a scale of 1-5, 5 being the greatest, how would I rate my self-esteem?

2. What forms of positive reinforcement will I take in?

3. What are some things a professional can help me sort out? How can I get connected with one?

4. What will I do regularly to ensure that I'm getting "me time"?

5. What sources of negative energy are in my life? How will I eliminate them?

6. What will I do to maintain my dignity?

CHAPTER SIX

REBUILD YOUR STRENGTH

My Voice
By Pamela A. Larde

My voice gives me strength. It is all my own.
This melodious voice that stutters to find its place,
That insists on standing up for me,
That shapes my inner being,
That exposes truths and sends fools running for cover,
My voice is relentless and unapologetic.
It inspires people to love me,
Challenges people to respect me,
And embraces the beauty that lives unapologetically within me,
This is my voice.

Letter 21

NUTS AND BOLTS OF STRENGTH

My Sister,

Managing to stay strong after a breakup isn't always easy. Sometimes it's a challenge to resist calling just to hear their voice, to resist settling because the loneliness is too overwhelming, or to resist lashing out in the heat of anger. Strength is key, but it does get difficult sometimes. In order to remain strong enough to resist calling, settling, or lashing out, it is essential to build strength as your foundation so that you become an all-around strong person. Trying to be strong enough to resist certain scenarios without working toward becoming a person with a strong disposition is like hustling backwards. This will never work in the long run. Rebuilding strength doesn't start with your actions, it starts with your mind. It's your mindset that influences your actions.

The weaker I am on the inside, the more difficult it is for me to resist giving in, or picking up the phone, or settling for whatever. Trying to leave Brian was like that constant battle between the devil on my left shoulder and the angel on my right. I didn't always know how to say no when he came back around, or how to exercise enough self-control to wait for the right situation. I was so insistent on marrying the father of my child that I lost sight of the reality that was sitting right before me. I didn't know that I could demand more for my life.

Once I figured out how to use my voice, and once I developed some self-control, I became much better at standing my ground when I was tempted to settle. I began to see right through the folly and foolishness that the devil on my left shoulder often presented to me, while I admired the truth and integrity that was spoken by the angel on my right.

Don't you hate those internal battles? When you just want something because you want it? You try to reason with yourself about why you have the right to have it and how you only live once, until finally, you give in. *Who cares? I'm doing me. I deserve this!* Yep. Been there. But the reality of it is that you're not doing you. You're *fooling* you. In the end, it's never worth it. Never. Especially if we're talking about a relationship that has officially ended and is not meant to be. Letting go takes strength.

So how do you rebuild your strength after you've been wide open, unguarded, fully exposed, and totally vulnerable? You rebuild strength by learning to use your voice and by developing self-control. Your voice is powerful. Not only does it tell other people where you stand and what you're all about, but your voice reinforces to *you* where you stand and what you're all about. Speaking it out loud gives strength to who you are and what you believe in.

Self-control is also pretty empowering. Even if you're not quite strong enough to resist all temptations, each time you successfully stand your ground and resist a temptation, you reinforce that stance to *yourself.* You grow a little stronger each time you successfully resist. Using your voice and exercising self-control both send a message to those who interact with you, but most importantly, these actions send a message to yourself. They strengthen you and help you actually see that you can do whatever it is you have set out to do. In the next letter, let's start with the power of your voice.

Love,

Dr. Pamela

whatever it is you have set out to do in the next letter. Let's start
with the power of your voice.

Love,

P. Pamela

Letter 22

THE POWER OF YOUR VOICE

My Sister,

It's time to take some voice lessons. Don't worry—you
won't need an angelic voice for these lessons. In fact, the
firmer and coarser you voice is, the better. When rebuilding
your strength, there are two very essential vocal skills to
focus on developing: your ability to say *no* to what you don't
want, and your willingness to say *yes* to what you do want.
That's it! It's that simple.

I don't know about you, but the primary reason why I was
in each of my unhealthy relationships for so long was
because I did neither of these two things. I accepted
whatever I got, and I hoped that because I was kind, the
relationships would eventually change into something I
wanted and deserved. I didn't say *no* because I thought my
boldness would tick them off, and I didn't say *yes* because I
thought what I wanted was too much to ask for. It was a
pretty pathetic way to exist in a relationship, but this is what
I thought it took to survive.

Even if this isn't exactly how it all went down for you, it's
important to strengthen your vocal skills so that next time
you find yourself in an unfulfilling, unhealthy, or simply not
meant to be situation, you'll be better equipped to use your

voice and ensure that your needs are met. Let's begin our lessons with the ability to say *no*.

SAYING NO

Being able to say no is important because this is how we stand up for ourselves. Some people are great at saying no. Others struggle immensely. I'm one of those who struggle because I am a notorious people pleaser. It was even worse when I had a weakened self-esteem, still raw and fresh out of a failed relationship. I wanted people to like me and to validate that going through a divorce didn't make me a bad person. I would often go out of my way to accommodate other people, even if it meant compromising myself, and even if it was an unreasonable burden. I also did this in each of my relationships. I compromised myself and carried them on long after I knew the relationship should have ended. I learned after my divorce that being able to say no and standing up for myself was an essential life skill that would make me a stronger and more respected person in all areas of my life.

If you don't stand up for yourself, who will? What are you teaching people about how to treat you if you don't stand up for yourself? Saying no means refusing to be treated with anything less than dignity and respect. It means refusing to compromise yourself to satisfy someone else. It means rejecting expectations that don't match your personal goals or values. Having the ability to say no is beneficial in every aspect of your life from your intimate relationships, to interactions with colleagues, to being a best friend. As you master the ability to say no in each area of your life, you gradually rebuild your strength and you will be well equipped to stand your ground and demand respect as you begin dating again.

Saying Yes

Another important way to use your voice is by being willing to say *yes* to what you do want and need in your life. This begins with first knowing what it is you want and need, then believing that you deserve what you want and need. If you don't know what you want or don't believe that you deserve it, you probably won't say yes to it when it is offered—and forget about stepping out on a limb to ask for it! Saying yes builds up your strength because it's just another way of standing up for yourself. It's another way of ensuring that you are being taken care of. Saying yes reaffirms to yourself and to others that you are worthy of having peace, happiness, and joy in your life.

If an awesome someone steps into your life and treats you like an absolute queen, welcome it! Say yes to it. Enjoy it. Love it. Just don't lose sight of what it is you are trying to accomplish by losing your bearings and falling head over heels before you're ready. That's a whole different road that I don't advise you going down at this time (take it from someone who's been there). Take everything slow but be willing to accept the good that comes to you. Get used to the good so that if anything not-so-good comes along, your instinct will be to avoid it at all costs.

Najee was the awesome someone who stepped into my life shortly after my divorce, and I learned for the very first time what it meant to be treated with total respect; to be listened to, complimented, and admired. My eyes were forever opened to what I never knew was possible. I had no idea that I could develop such a friendship with a man or that I could ever be treasured the way that I had been with Najee. He was very clear about setting boundaries, as we were both going through changes at that point, but I was no fool. What that man was offering as a friend was exactly what I needed. For the first time, I realized that what I had experienced in the past did not have to define my future. So I said yes. *Hell yes.* Show me what it means to feel beautiful, to be loved, to be someone's best friend, to be fully respected. Girl, that man turned my whole life around, just by showing me what I had been missing, all because I said yes to what I wanted and needed. In no way do I regret his presence in my life or the time we spent together. Indeed, I am a better person because of it.

If something comes your way—a new companion, an act of kindness, a spa day for yourself, whatever it is—if it makes you feel great about yourself, if it makes you feel like a queen, don't be afraid to say yes. You deserve it! Don't just sit around and wait for other people to bring that something to you. If you say yes to yourself, and yes to happiness, and yes to having your wants and needs fulfilled, the people in your life will admire you for it. You'll attract people into your life who respect you and who want to treat you exactly the way you are treating yourself. But you have to know what you want and believe that you deserve it.

There's just one caveat to this yes thing. Be sure that your yeses are yeses that will move you forward, that are healthy for you, and that will not take you down a road of distraction. The purpose of saying yes is to improve your life, not to return to what you are trying to come out of. Be smart and real with yourself about your wants and needs. Be sure that they are wants and needs that are truly in your best interests.

By learning how to say no and standing up for yourself, and by being willing to say yes to what you want and need, you are shaping the value of your relationships and how people treat and respect you. This is a powerful way to rebuild your strength and lay the foundation for a future of amazingly fulfilling relationships. Stand up for yourself and choose those things that bring you joy. You'll be amazed at how much more power and control you will have in your life.

Muah,

Dr. Pamela

Letter 23

THE POWER OF SELF-CONTROL

My Sister,

The final strategy I recommend for rebuilding your strength is developing self-control. Much like what is needed to rebuild muscles and physical strength, this strategy takes practice, perseverance, and patience. The most effective way to develop and strengthen self-control is by practicing it. The goal is to become a fully self-controlled person in all areas of your life. You don't want to become that person who gives in to excessive unhealthy indulgences because you don't know how not to indulge, or because you don't feel like knowing how. This is a very passive and uncontrolled way of living and will in no way help you build your strength. Self-control, if truly mastered, is a skill that a person fully embodies. It takes real commitment to achieve it.

I realize that in my last letter to you, I told you to *enjoy, say yes, be happy,* and all that jazz. I still mean that, but this is where it is up to you to decipher between reasonable indulgences and indulgences that are self-destructive. Let's use food as an example. Having a candy bar every once in awhile can be a reasonable indulgence because it tastes good, it's personally satisfying, and it can be a small way of treating yourself. Having that candy bar every day, on the other hand, can be self-destructive. Lacking self-control makes you weaker. This does nothing for rebuilding your strength.

By all means, treat yourself to what you enjoy. Just do this under control. Be wise about whether or not what you enjoy is what you *need* and what you can handle. I mean, let's be real… My preference as a healthy sexual being is not to be celibate, *ever*. But during each of these transitional times in my life, while I was in the process of letting go, sex as a Band-Aid was the last thing I *needed*. It would've made things much worse for me in the long run. Everyone's threshold is different. Everyone's needs and wants are different, so I'm definitely not going to tell you what you should and should not do. Just be real with yourself about what you need and what should and should not be an indulgence in your life.

The key to being in control is to practice it so that you can become a fully self-controlled person. What I mean by this is that it's not enough that you resisted picking up the phone to call him all of last week. That's a great accomplishment, but you'll know that you've arrived when you find that you're self-controlled in *all* areas of your life. This includes not taking in a gallon of ice cream in one sitting, not getting sloppy drunk to numb the pain, and not settling for a someone who is a bad fit for you just because you are sick of being alone. Becoming a self-controlled person means that you are patient, that you persevere until you are successful, and that you refuse to settle.

Patience

Patience is by far one of the most difficult qualities that I have worked on developing in myself. I hate having to be patient. I'm a control freak, so if I want something to happen, I want it to happen *today*. Right now. And if I can't make it happen right now with my own two hands, I try to orchestrate some grandiose scheme to ensure that it does happen. And when that fails (because it always does when it isn't meant to be), I go crazy and throw pity party tantrums. My masterful orchestration skills are precisely what got me married to Jackson. I was obsessively impatient and refused to take the time to read the many signs that lay before me. He told me and showed me in numerous ways that he wasn't ready, but I didn't want to start over with someone new, so I did everything in my power to make it happen with him—and it *did* happen. He married me! I soon realized, however, that my orchestration skills had failed me once again.

Patience definitely was not my forte. I hated waiting so much that I would intentionally arrive late to meetings and get-togethers just to avoid that awful experience of having to wait. I know...horrible. I still struggle with patience sometimes, but I'm not nearly as bad as I used to be. This is largely because (thanks to my life processors) I finally took notice of the destruction that my lack of patience has caused. I opened my eyes and began to see the pattern of chaos that trailed each of my impatient outbursts. This realization compelled me to develop more patience. I desperately wanted my life to change for the better, so I practiced it. I started small by developing new habits, like arriving early to meetings and get-togethers to experience what it means to wait, and you know what? It really wasn't that horrible. If you're one of those people who like to arrive early anyway, you probably think I'm nuts. Once I discovered how in control I felt by arriving early—how much calmer I felt, how much more prepared I was—my perspective changed.

For larger goals, I learned to focus on smaller endeavors that would bring me closer to achieving the larger goal. Remember the credit issue I wrote about in Letter 19? A year after my divorce was final, I had my heart set on buying my own house in a neighborhood with a bunch of kids and a cluster of good schools. Unfortunately, my credit had been so badly damaged by the divorce process that buying a house was a laughable goal to the many lenders I reached out to for approval (some of them were just flat-out mean). This seemed to be totally out of my hands, and I was thoroughly frustrated by it all. At the time, the kids and I were living with my parents and I had a fifty-mile commute to work. I wanted desperately to have my own place and to live closer to my job. *Now. RIGHT NOW.*

But throwing tantrums didn't work. And being pissed off didn't work. I needed to fix my credit. There was no way around that one. I resolved that I had no other choice but to be patient and focus on a smaller, more immediate goal. And that's what I did. I focused on paying off all of my credit cards—one by one, month by month. By acknowledging the different scenarios in my life that I could not immediately change, I found ways to practice patience by accepting what I could not control and taking charge of what I could. Patience and control go hand-in-hand.

This strategy has really helped me to realize that I *am* in control because everything I do today affects the outcome of tomorrow. If I do something crazy and rash because I just couldn't wait, I may reap what I think is an immediate reward, when actually, it was never a reward at all—just a temporary illusion of happiness. If I stay in control, accept what I cannot immediately change, and prepare myself to be ready for what I want, my rewards will be much greater and more enduring. This is true control. This is what helps us to become more self-controlled inside and out.

Perseverance

Self-control is also developed through perseverance. This means that you are in it for the long haul and that your patience doesn't wear out after facing what seems to be a relentless string of challenges. Fasting, I've learned, is a great way to practice perseverance. I gave it a try for the first time a year after my divorce with hopes that I could find some clarity and experience a new level of spiritual growth. I was just about at the point of utter frustration with the fact that I was single with no prospects when my pastor initiated this twenty-one-day fast. The timing was perfect. I had seriously been toying with the idea of just settling for any guy who was breathing and showed interest. I was sick of being alone all of the time. New city, no friends, no social life. Total frustration.

I decided to do the fast. It was a flexible one. My pastor gave the congregation several options to accommodate the different levels of faith represented: a no foods after six p.m. fast, an all fruits and veggies fast, and a liquids-only fast. I have never been an avid veggie eater, so I thought it would be a great challenge for me—a way to practice overcoming a terrible life-long fear of these incredibly healthy foods. I did pretty well for a first-timer. I spent Sunday evenings planning my meals for the week. I'd make sure the refrigerator was well stocked with the staples. I knew myself all too well. If I ran out of veggies and was caught hungry, I would undoubtedly wolf down some chicken, candy, or fries in the midst of my weakness. The strategy worked, and I managed to stay on track—for the most part. I'll admit I did slip up once, but what I learned from the experience was priceless. A commitment like fasting takes much more than patience. It takes strategy, planning, and serious discipline. It takes perseverance.

People who have completed a college degree, or who have raised children alone, or who have crossed the finish line in a marathon know what it means to persevere. They had a goal in mind and actively overcame the challenges along the way until that goal was achieved. When they wanted to quit, they kept going. When one direction didn't work, they chose another. The pain didn't stop them. The exhaustion didn't deter them. They just kept going. This is perseverance. Once you've persevered through something, you know that you have great capacity for self-control. The more you persevere, the more self-control you develop, and the more self-control you develop, the more you rebuild your strength. So find ways—as many ways as possible—to practice perseverance. Run a marathon. Participate in a fast. Raise some kids. Take control.

Never Settle

Finally, I want to remind you to resist any urge to settle. This goes for anything and everything that you have your heart set on. Remain patient and keep persevering until you get exactly what it is you want, need, and deserve. When I was in this highly vulnerable place in my life, it just so happened that several super-handsome, accomplished *married* men started hitting on me, all at the same time. *What's up with that?* I have to admit that the compliments and offers were flattering. But I was not about to reduce myself to settling for something that would only bring more complication into my life, not to mention the great harvest (or karma) I might reap from messing around with someone else's husband. *No way.* I definitely didn't need *that* hanging over my head. Settling for whatever comes your way is a sure sign of weakness and will significantly break down, rather than build up, your strength.

Hold on to that backbone of yours. Rebuilding strength is by no means an easy task, but it is crucial to your ability to let go and move forward with your life. Strength enables you to stand your ground, stay focused, and go after all that you want and need to live the life you deserve. Giving in to your weaknesses will send you flying in the opposite direction.

I challenge you to get creative. Think about what you'll need to do to develop self-control. In what areas of your life do you struggle to stay disciplined? Do you have a hard time resisting foods that are bad for you? Do you exercise regularly? Do you have a knack for gossip? Do you sleep too much? Whatever it is—challenge yourself to get disciplined in that area. Come up with creative and strategic ways of resisting what you shouldn't do, and begin doing what you need to do for your well-being.

Remember, developing self-control means much more than having self-controlled moments. It's about becoming a self-controlled *person*. It's about being disciplined enough to manage all areas of your life without giving in to excessive, self-destructive indulgences. Knowing that you've become a master of self-control helps you hold your head high in confidence. Each time you are successfully patient, each time you persevere, and each time you refuse to settle, you add building blocks to your strength. Practice as much as possible, and one day, you will wake up and realize that you truly are a strong person. Trust me. It can work!

Love you,

Dr. Pamela

♥ INSPIRE YOUR HEART

1. What do I not need in my life right now?

2. How will I go about resisting those things that I don't need in my life?

3. How will I communicate my boundaries to others who try to push me toward what I don't need?

4. What are some positive steps I can take in order to receive what I do need and deserve?

CHAPTER SEVEN

REBUILD TRUST

The moment we have a negative experience, we get stuck in what was done and how it was done to us. We must learn not to take life so personally. People are not really out to get us. Let us learn to give up anger and fear by replacing those things with love.

\- Iyanla Vanzant
Facebook Post, November 11, 2012

Letter 24

GOOD RELATIONSHIPS EXIST

My Sister,

When I think back, I am amazed by how many people took great measures to explain to me that my dream of finding a loving and fulfilling relationship was nothing more than fairytale thinking. Their messages were harmonic: All men cheat. The good ones are gone. I have to lower my standards to get what I really want. *Really?* Think about that for a second. Lower my standards to get what I want? Now there's an oxymoron if I've ever heard one! These are the messages that continued to resonate from the mouths of other women who had been hurt and wanted to offer me their sage advice. What they were really doing, however, was attempting to project their own fears and insecurities about love onto me. I wasn't having it.

I'm grateful for my hard-headed determination to get what I want. I refused to believe these voices. I refused to allow myself to fall into hopeless ways of thinking. What did I have to lose by choosing to believe in love? Believing in love kept me positive and healthy. Because of this chosen mindset, I drew other positive and healthy people into my life and kept the negative and life-sucking people out—for the most part.

After I moved to Atlanta, I experienced a year of no dating. Not because I didn't want to date, but because every guy I met seemed to have a negative life-sucking vibe that so opposed my entire way of thinking and living that I could never even make it past one conversation with them. It's that natural process of elimination I mentioned in Letter 11. Those who don't mesh well with you will weed themselves out naturally if you don't step in the way of the process.

It was definitely a discouraging year. Had I decided to take on that angry, bitter mentality, there may have actually been some chemistry between these guys and myself—dangerous, co-dependent chemistry. But because they were not looking for what I was looking for and because they were of a totally different mentality, they seemed to drop like flies. I didn't even make it to a first date with any of these guys. There were times when I would find myself utterly frustrated about not meeting anyone, but I soon came to realize that I was being protected from drama, bad relationships, and wounded guys who wouldn't do me any good. Protected because I was dead set on believing that true love exists, that I was going to find it, and that I would not allow the bad choices I had made in the past affect the amazing future that was ahead of me. I didn't want to lose my ability to trust in someone who would love me the way I knew I could be loved. I did eventually begin meeting people who had mindsets that were more compatible to mine. They still believed in love. They wanted love. They wanted to trust and to be trustworthy. This kept me encouraged. It was a reminder that I was on the right path.

What's your mindset like right now? How have you been thinking these days? What you allow yourself to believe dictates your life. Are you setting yourself up to welcome more drama into your life? Are you stuck in a state of anger, mistrust, and negative thinking? Have you fallen into the mindset that your dreams are nothing more than unrealistic or unattainable fantasies? Do you believe that you'll have to settle for less than you deserve and desire in order to find love? Or are you climbing upward? I finally decided that two bad relationships were more than enough. It was time to refuse to allow what I had experienced before into my life again. I knew what I had to offer and I decided that I would only offer what I have to someone who was worthy of it and who was willing to offer the same.

What does all of this have to do with trust? Trust begins with your mindset. It begins with what's inside of you. It's all about how you think. When I say that you should rebuild (or build) the ability to trust, I am not saying that you should become naïve and believe everything you hear. I am saying that you should adopt a mentality that still believes in love. Trust cannot exist without love. If you don't believe in love, you won't be inspired to trust anyone. It begins with what you believe about love and what you believe you can have in your life. Once your beliefs change, your life can change. You'll carry yourself differently. You'll look better. You'll feel better. You'll quickly drive away negative-thinking people and attract those who think and live the way you do. People who live their lives in love and trust want to surround themselves with people who also love and trust. When you get to this place of truly believing in love, it will be easier to trust because you can more easily recognize who is and is not trustworthy. As a loving and trusting individual, you train yourself to recognize what love and trust look, feel, and taste like.

The first step to trusting is learning how to trust the process—the process of letting go, of struggle, of being alone, of not knowing what lies ahead for you. It is inevitable that you

188   PAMELA A. LARDE

advance through each phase of this process before reaching the next level of your life. Trust that this process is not designed to ruin your life or keep you away from love and companionship. In fact, it is designed to move you into the direction of love, because for whatever reason, you were not headed that way before you stepped into this great life transition we call heartbreak. When you learn to trust the process, your entire outlook changes. You realize that what you are experiencing today is for a greater purpose. As much as this may hurt at the moment, the ability to trust the process can provide you with the strength you need to keep moving forward.

Inherent in the ability to trust the process is knowing that good relationships do exist and that you can have one of those for yourself. Good relationships aren't just something we see on TV. They are real. We just have to expect to have one for ourselves. It's no different than searching for a job. The candidate who is proactive does her research, is confident that there is something out there for her, and prepares herself to be the most desirable applicant. She is much more likely to get the job than the candidate who approaches the search with hopelessness, who questions whether or not she's good enough, is convinced that she'll never find the job she really wants, or believes that she's destined to be unemployed for years to come. If she wants the job, she must first believe that there are many opportunities out there for her—and that one of those opportunities will one day be hers.

My sister, if you ever expect to find yourself in a loving, fulfilling relationship, you must know with all of your heart that these relationships do exist, and that you will have one—not that there's more women in the world than men or that people just aren't faithful anymore. Scratch that rhetoric out of your head and focus on what you *will* have. If you're not there yet, you can get there by being intentional about it. This doesn't happen overnight, nor does it happen passively. You have to train yourself to believe it by educating yourself and by giving thanks for what is to come of your life.

Educate Yourself

Take the time to educate yourself. Find out what loving and fulfilling relationships look like. Talk to people who are in them. If you don't know of any, *seek out* people who are in them. Talk to these couples. Learn their stories of love, romance, triumph, good days and bad days, and how they came to where they are today. Take the time to explore real stories about successful relationships. What hard lessons did they learn? What can you learn from their experiences? Surround yourself with positive examples, while politely avoiding the negative ones. Think about what you personally want and need in your next relationship. What you want may be very different than what your best friend, your mother, or your sister wants. Perhaps you are not an overly affectionate person and would be put off by a person who is. Or maybe you dream of a partner who will pray with you, or who makes eye contact when speaking with you, or who makes you laugh uncontrollably. What do you want and on what will you absolutely not compromise? You have to know these things so that you'll recognize what you want when you see it—and then *believe* that what you desire is out there for you. If you operate from the mindset that it's out there, you'll find it.

Give Thanks

One of the greatest gifts that came out of my time with Najee was that for the first time, I experienced what it felt like to be genuinely admired by someone—to have someone look into my eyes when I spoke as if nothing in the world mattered, to have someone take my hands at a restaurant and pray together over the meal, to have someone tell me that I was beautiful. I never knew so much love and respect between a man and a woman were possible. Once I felt the euphoria of that, there was no turning back. What I took with me was the desire to feel that way again. After my experience with Najee, I was unwilling to settle for anything less. I knew that I wasn't exposed to this experience for nothing. I knew that this was but a taste of what was to come for me, so I looked forward to finding it wholly and completely.

In anticipation and preparation for the love that I knew was going to come into my life, I began to give thanks early. I thought about what I really wanted out of a relationship and visualized myself receiving all of it. Eventually, I began to speak out my grateful expectations:

Thank you for helping me find this place of peace in my life.
Thank you for sending a life companion who will love me.
Thank you for the moments that they will put their arms around me and kiss my face.
Thank you for their desire to play with my hair.
Thank you for the belly laughs we'll have together.
Thank you for the peace we will find in one another.

I could go on and on. The more I did that—especially on my most difficult, hopeless days—the more I came to believe this truly would happen for me. These thank-you moments would have me smiling from ear to ear, not much different from the smile I donned as I walked across the stage on my graduation day two years earlier.

There is a caveat to this. Don't consume yourself with a quest to find new love. Don't try to rush this very important period of your life. This is your time to prepare for your next chapter, which includes much, much more than finding love. I've talked about how impatient I am. I constantly had to check myself about wanting to rush this part along. I had many moments of frustration over being single for what I considered to be too long. But I had many ways (and a few friends) to keep myself in check when I'd hit a woe-is-me moment. At this point, it wasn't so much about missing the exes as it was about wanting to just move forward with someone new in my life. Forget the process. I wanted what I wanted when I wanted it.

But experience taught me better. I knew that rushing things would only set me right back into another unhealthy or unfulfilling relationship. So I focused on identifying what I actually did want in my life. When I felt discouraged, I went down my mental list of "thank-yous" for what I knew was to come in my life: *Thank you for the joy of love that I am being prepared for. Thank you for protecting me from foolishness. Thank you for the life testimony that is unfolding on this very day.* Through this practice of giving thanks, I was able to adopt a grateful mindset that kept me more focused on the positive possibilities than the negative what-ifs.

Prepare Yourself

Once I came to a place where I truly believed that there were good relationships out there and that I would one day have one of my own, it was time to get myself ready to receive what I wanted. When love arrived, I didn't want to be so unprepared that I would unknowingly let it pass me by.

Prepare yourself. Take the time to understand what you need, and then get ready for it. Carefully unpack your baggage and let it go. Avoid projecting your negative experiences of the past onto the person who could become the love of your life. Be willing to trust people, rather than always assuming the worst. An unjustifiable lack of trust is a sign of past trauma creeping into the present. Some people should absolutely be avoided—this is true—but if your mind, all people are untrustworthy at all times, your relationships won't stand a chance, as no relationship can thrive if it is riddled with mistrust and fear. Good relationships are out there, my sister, and if you're willing to allow yourself to trust this process and to trust that you will have a good relationship in due time, the heart stretching you are experiencing today will not be in vain.

Start thinking about what you want the next phase of your life to look like. Does it include new love? Is it all about your career? Will you travel? Whatever it is, figure out what you want and start moving in that direction by educating yourself and by giving thanks for what is coming in your life. You can have it. You just have to start believing it.

This is not all there is to developing the ability to trust, especially if your last relationship involved any element of betrayal. How do you bounce back from that? How do you know when your instincts are talking and if they're correct? In my next letter, we'll touch upon betrayal, its detrimental effect on trust, and how you can address it proactively. Things are about to get heavy, my sister!

Love,

Dr. Pamela

Letter 25

THE ANATOMY OF BETRAYAL

My Sister,

I realize that all relationships don't end as a result of betrayal, so I definitely don't want to assume that this is what happened in your case. But understanding how the dynamics of betrayal play out and how to rebuild a sense of trust after it happens is a lesson that each us can benefit from, especially as we prepare to experience dating again.

It took quite some time for me to realize and accept that Jackson's decision to sneak around behind my back was not my fault. He betrayed my trust as a result of the personal issues he was dealing with. When we met, he was heartbroken from a previous relationship, so he threw up a wall to protect himself from being hurt by the next woman who came along—me. I spent many years blaming myself, apologizing after arguments, and trying to "work on myself" so that he would see that I was a good person, worthy of his love and faithfulness. I had one thing right: I was a good person. But I had it twisted when I believed that I needed to prove to him that I was worthy of his love. My worthiness had long been proven in my integrity, loyalty, and faithfulness as a friend. It was he who should have been working tirelessly to do the proving because it was he who lacked integrity, loyalty, and faithfulness in our relationship.

How is it that I got so caught up and so flipped upside down that I could rationalize this kind of thinking: *He lied to me and betrayed my trust. Now it's up to me to salvage this relationship. I'm going to kick it into high gear and be the best woman I can be so that he'll want to do better.* How did that logic actually compute in my brain? I'm a pretty bright and analytical chick, but somehow, in the midst of my desperation, this line of thinking made perfect sense to me for an entire decade. Oh, the things we do to be loved!

I'm not the only woman guilty of this. Women tell me stories all the time about how they tried to hang in there for an unfaithful partner. They felt strongly that it was their responsibility to help them through some rough patch in their life and to give him a chance to become a better person—all because they said they wanted to change.

Of course they said they wanted to change. Why do heart feelers like myself (I'll just speak for myself) feel take this on as if this is our responsibility? We don't owe them this level of devotion that requires us to compromise our own dignity and self-respect. It took a decade for me to realize that I needed to let Jackson go and heal on his own. What he was dealing with was between God and himself—and God didn't ask me to play middle woman. They both needed me to get the hell out of the way.

Here's what is happening in the mind of a betrayer while you're hanging in there with all your might. They're experiencing the best of both worlds—the freedom to indulge in whatever it is they have to lie to you about, and the security that no matter what they do (or don't do), you'll be there as a pillar of strength for them. Of course, they would prefer not to get caught and not to have to deal with the dramatic discussions to follow, but if they do get caught, they know in the end that you're going to be there to give them the love, support, and time they need to get their act together—however long that may be. You may be angry. You may scream and shout. You may cry. You may even end the relationship. But they knows you'll be back, so there's never any real incentive to get their act together completely—just enough to keep you *barely* satisfied. They can act up and still keep this good woman? Change for what? Change is too difficult, too scary, too uncomfortable, so why bother? Once they've got you there, betrayal is easy. And someone who is not ready to change will choose women who are easily betrayed—because there's little pressure to do anything differently.

Until all of this made sense to me, I believed that Jackson was unfaithful because I wasn't enough—not pretty enough, not cool enough, not daring enough. I thought I was pushing him away by complaining too much or by putting too much pressure on him. I resolved that if I wanted him to change, I had to behave differently—stay off his case and love him harder. But this only added fuel to his betrayal. I was essentially helping this man betray me. No matter how much I spoke up or bit my tongue, how much I supported him, or how diligently I gave him what he wanted, absolutely nothing seemed to change—until the day I told myself: *It's not me. It's him. He's the one who needs to change.* I just needed to step out of the way.

But this epiphany wasn't enough. I wasn't off the hook yet. While Jackson's behavior may not have been my fault, the fact that I allowed him to be there totally was. The type of people I allow in my life, the baggage I agree to help them carry, and the treatment I put up with is entirely up to me. Here's the distinction: his personal issues and consequential betrayal are not elements of the relationship that I caused or deserved. Because of this, I could not change that behavior. Only he could.

What I could have changed, however, was my choice to nurture the behavior. I could have changed the role and level of significance he played in my life. I can decide whom I allow to dwell in my space, and I can change my mind about that decision anytime I choose to.

Now that you're out of your situation, it's important to discover ways to reduce the odds that you'll experience a betrayal-laden relationship in the future—even if the one you just left involved no betrayal. There is no way to guarantee that no one will ever lie to you. We can't control the actions of other people, but we can keep the betrayal target off of our backs and make our expectations abundantly clear. The key is to tackle any questionable behavior at the outset. Once we have sent the message that inconsistency, disrespect, or shady behavior is okay, it is really difficult to reverse the course of that relationship later.

Remove the Target

People who practice betrayal as a way of life have a pretty good idea of whom they can deceive. They are drawn to people who won't challenge them too much—or who won't stand their ground if they do try to initiate a challenge. Betrayers are drawn to people who are intimidated by them. They seek out emotionally dependent people who will accept just anyone in their lives for fear of being alone. This makes it easy for the betrayer to live multiple lives without much challenge to change. The lower the self-esteem and sense of personal control in the unsuspecting victim, the better for the betrayer.

Remove that target. Your first line of defense is to be a threat to those who practice deception. It's okay to love and trust, but it's important to be wise and to use discretion when doing so. Everyone you meet and adore doesn't deserve your all. In fact, *most* people you meet will not qualify to receive your all because all people will not be the right fit for you. Be wise by paying attention to the patterns. Use discretion by taking the time to actually get to know who it is you're dealing with.

The Web Search

These days, with a wealth of information at our fingertips, it has become common practice to turn to the Internet for help in determining whether or not we have a betrayer on our hands. Even with all of this access to information, I can't emphasize enough the power of plain, good old-fashioned getting to know someone by *listening and paying attention.* Google would not have told me that Brian and Jackson were each not a good fit for me, that one was emotionally unstable and that the other was sneaking across the street for secret rendezvous with our gorgeous neighbor—but my instincts surely told me.

You may very well get lucky and uncover the scandal of the year by doing an efficient internet search, but anything you find can be rationalized away if you're already vulnerable. Betrayers are experts at this, so don't let this replace your God-given gift of intuition. Keep your eyes open and pay attention. Be wise. And don't become obsessed. There's quite a difference between a basic web search to ensure safety and flat-out obsession or paranoia over someone's life.

A betrayer knows this difference. They will welcome the paranoid, fearful, and insecure woman into their world with open arms because their comforting words are all it will take to calm her down. She just wants to be comforted. She wants what feels good—even if it really isn't good. The wise and discretionary woman on the other hand? She requires authentic goodness, not just what feels good. A betrayer will recognize her a mile away and will avoid her at all costs. That's exactly what you want—to keep them at a distance!

Be You

I once had a conversation with a young woman frustrated over a situation in which her kindness had been taken for granted. She bitterly announced that she would simply stop being such a nice person. I totally understood where she was coming from. I have declared the same words myself on more than one occasion, but what I've come to realize is that it's much more rewarding to be true to who you are than to be something else. I was not created with a kind and caring personality just to cover all of that up. Over time, I've learned how to strike the balance between being kind and caring while protecting myself from those who were not. I have to be myself. Growing a thick skin came in time, but I had to stay the course and be true to who I was in order to get there.

What I'm saying to you, my sister, is that removing your target does not require that you replace the "nice you" with a "hard-core, grunting you." It just means that you protect yourself from those who have ill intentions. Rather than rely solely on your internet investigations or assume that everyone is out to betray you, learn how to read people and their actions to determine who should and should not be trusted. I now have an incredible amount of unshakable strength when it comes to backing away from someone whose behaviors and intentions are questionable. If it doesn't feel right, I'm gone. By all means, be nice, but balance that with a healthy dose of don't-mess-with-me assertiveness.

If you are a kind and caring person by nature, please don't attempt to transform into something hard-core as a strategy for warding off the betrayers. This is not protecting yourself. This is a manifestation of bitterness. Becoming bitter will set you further back than just being who you are ever could. Embrace who you are and tolerate no less than the treatment you deserve.

Bottom line—betrayal is the betrayer's problem, not yours. Once you've realized this and have removed yourself from the situation, it's up to you to stand firm.

Love you,

Dr. Pamela

Letter 26

OPEN YOURSELF UP

My Sister,

Going through a breakup can leave us stressed out, uptight, and walking around with clenched fists, closed up by anger and fear. The problem with this is that a clenched fist is unable to release what it is clinging to and is closed too tightly to receive anything new. If you live this way long enough, your hands will begin to cramp and may even get locked into place.

It's time to relax. Find ways to let loose and release so that you are not living in high stress mode on a day-to-day basis. Relax so that you are more pleasant and approachable to people you may want in your life. Relax so that you can be open enough to receive what you deserve. I realize that the very thought of opening yourself up can be a scary one, but if you have taken refocusing and rebuilding seriously, you are well on your way. You've taken the time to take care of yourself, so this final step—trust—is the last piece to master before learning how to love again.

Opening up means believing that there is greatness out there just waiting for you, and that you're open to exploring what that is. I know so many people who are afraid of the unknown and only live within their own narrowly defined boundaries. I know of friends who have had excellent opportunities but were too afraid to pursue them because the job was out of state, they had two kids, or the competition was just too intimidating.

When you're closed, you risk missing out on some of life's greatest opportunities. Opening up means embracing new opportunities, new places, new friendships, and new experiences. Now that you are out of your relationship, this is the time to rediscover who you are, what you enjoy, and who best complements your personality. This is the time to explore. Cut your hair. Travel to a different country. Join a new group. Change your wardrobe. Pursue a different career. Try an online dating service. I did all of these things—the most dramatic of which was cutting twelve inches of length from my locks. I woke up one morning with locks that flowed down my back and went to bed that night totally free—with a short bob that rested just above my ears. Yes, I went dramatic! I embraced change like it was my one-way ticket to happiness.

Opening myself up to life's possibilities was by far one of the greatest gifts I granted myself after I left Jackson. I made some awesome friends, finally took that trip to Jamaica, moved out of the state to take the job of my dreams, changed my wardrobe, and bought a new house. The list goes on and on. I would not have recognized myself years earlier. When I was with Jackson, I lived to survive—to merely get through each day. My big dreams were but a distant memory because to pursue them would have meant rocking the boat, and our boat was already so fragile. I wanted to keep Jackson calm. I feared every day that he was going to leave me, so I lived very carefully. I also wanted to keep the tension between him and my son from coming to a head. I wanted peace in our home, so I took my steps carefully to maintain the balance between my overwhelming life as mother, student, professional, and wife. We were so fragile, one hiccup could cause all of that to come crashing down. My mind couldn't conceive of thinking beyond the limited walls of our little world. I lived in fear, numbness, and a constant state of instability.

When I finally left Jackson, everything almost instantly changed. I loved the woman I became. I laughed more. I looked better. I felt more in charge. I was more in tune with myself, and I had more confidence than ever before. Being open and willing to try new things, using my voice, and exploring new avenues changed my life. Suddenly, anything was possible. After reaching this amazing new height in life, there was no turning back. I had a taste of the good life and I wasn't about to let that go.

There is much that awaits you. Don't be afraid of the possibilities. Find ways to step outside of your normal patterns and your comfort zone. Walk a new path to see where it takes you. Resist the urge to clamp up and close yourself off to the rest of the world. Unclench those fists. Open them up, shake them out, and lift your hands high to the heavens. Get ready to release the stress and receive the abundance of life that lies ahead for you.

Love,

Dr. Pamela

Letter 27

WHERE TO DRAW THE LINE

My Sister,

After all of this talk about trust, I've got one final piece of advice...Don't overdo it. There exists a thin line between trust and naïveté—a line between being open-minded and being a pushover. Remember your values. After leaving Jackson, I worked hard to become a strong and self-aware woman who was able to spot someone up to no good from a mile away. I trusted people, but I was much more discerning than I had ever been before. If it didn't feel right, I backed away. This is why I went dateless for so long. The vast majority of the guys I met after my divorce would have been a stretch for me. I would have had to settle for less than what I desired and deserved to even go on the date. Why would I walk into a situation that offers less than I desire and deserve from the jump? There's also a thin line between being open to receive and being willing to settle.

My time with Brian and Jackson taught me never to settle for less respect than I deserve. Never compromise my dignity and my values out of fear of being alone. Never lose sight of who I am and what I love. I learned to listen to my instincts and that they don't lie. If it doesn't look right, feel right, or smell right, it probably ain't right. I became a pro at moving on. No explanation needed. I don't owe anyone an explanation for what my instincts tell me. Once I learned to trust my instincts, I stopped doubting myself and found confidence in my ability to make sound decisions.

As you work on developing the ability to trust again, be sure that you maintain the integrity of who you are and who you would like to become. The key is to strike a balance. You don't want to open up too much too soon, yet you don't want to be too closed. When you find your balance somewhere in the middle, you are less likely to return to where you were before. This is where your growth begins.

The Power of Instinct

I am sure you have heard the expression, "follow your heart." Well, this isn't just about following some magical path to true love. Following your heart is another way of saying trust your instincts. Listen to what that voice within (your heart) is telling you. If you are having a conversation with a co-worker, for example, and suddenly you get the sense that they can't be trusted, listen. If someone you just met shows you a side of them that makes you raise an eyebrow and you have a feeling that something just ain't right, unless you're their therapist, you don't owe them the courtesy of sticking around to find out exactly what's not right. Just follow your heart and move on.

We were built with an internal alert system that signals certain alarms when we may be embarking upon a bad situation. The hairs on the back of our necks stand up. We feel rubbed the wrong way. We find no peace in anything this person says. Too often, we don't listen to these signals and move forward anyway. Sometimes, only in hindsight do we realize the mistake, but sometimes, hindsight is just too late. Your heart (or your instincts) keep you balanced so that you don't believe everything you hear—or find suspicion in everyone you meet. When you learn how to listen to your instincts, you should find yourself sitting at a healthy midpoint between the two extremes of being naïve and being paranoid.

THE TRUST SCALE

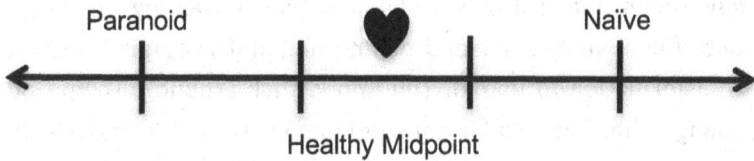

Paranoid   ♥   Naïve

Healthy Midpoint

Where do you think you would land on The Trust Scale? Do you often worry that people are out to deceive you? Or are you more likely to ignore the signs and plunge forward with hopes that things will just work out? Following your heart means that you don't have to keep tabs on someone's every move, and you also don't have to force yourself to believe something that is highly questionable. Following your heart keeps you somewhere right in the middle.

Too often we kick our instincts to the curb. When something isn't sitting well with us, we let other people tell us that we're overreacting, or we talk ourselves into believing that whatever isn't right will simply change. We cannot truly achieve trust if we haven't yet learned to trust our instincts. Your instinct is that voice that tells you whether or not something or someone should be trusted. If you don't know how to hear that voice and heed its warnings, there's no telling what you may walk into— or what you may fail to walk away from.

Jackson is a prime example of my unwillingness to follow instinct. In fact, not only did my instinct tell me to run, friends and family (including his!) also told me to run before we got married. I can count seven individuals at various points in our relationship who sat me down with grave concern to carefully explain why they believed in their hearts that Jackson was not the one for me. Even *their* instincts were working on my behalf! I responded by carefully explaining to each of them that I had already worked this out with God, that God was working on smoothing out Jackson's kinks, and that it was my duty as a faith-filled woman to stand behind him and wait for this great transformation to unfold. You know, stick around to help God change him. I was so far gone, no one even tried to argue with me. I had stomped my poor little voice of instinct so deep into the concrete, rational thinking of any kind was just not an option. My trust scale was terribly unbalanced. I was *all the way* to the right—about as naïve as they come.

My moment of truth reared its ugly head very early on. It was the very first time I caught Jackson in a lie, just two months after he and I met in college. I was out running errands on his side of town and thought I'd just swing by before I headed back home. I called his phone to give him a head's up, but he didn't answer. I decided to stop by anyway to surprise him. As I pulled up, I saw a girl leaving his house but thought nothing of it. He lived with four other guys, and I was sure girls were coming in and out of the place all the time. Besides, she appeared to be Asian, and as far as I knew, he only dated Black girls. In hindsight, however, I should have wondered why he was acting so shifty and restless when he opened the door. We sat in his bedroom and made awkward small talk until he got up to use the bathroom. He was acting so strange. *No affection at all? Was he even happy to see me? Maybe I shouldn't have come by.* I looked down at the floor casually, and my heart nearly stopped. Right there at my feet was a freshly used condom. *This is not happening...*Everything stopped at that moment. I felt so betrayed, angry, and hurt, I wanted to disappear. Suddenly everything made sense. No wonder he was so uptight! When I confronted him about it, he cried and begged and promised that he would change his ways. He lamented over how badly he wanted to be faithful to me, and that if I would just give him a chance, he would prove it to me.

Sure that I would never talk to him again, I left in tears. I told him to lose my number and refused to accept any explanation or apology he offered. I responded in exactly the way I was supposed to—at first. A couple of weeks of no contact went by before the phone calls began. Again, he begged and he promised. And then...he tapped into my weakness. He asked for my help. Help him become a better man. Help him become the man he's always wanted to be.

And that's what suckered me in. I am a helper. I want to believe in the best of people. The combination of those two amazing qualities is ultimately what compelled me to give Jackson another chance—to eventually hang around long enough to marry him six years later, and to stay married to him through five years of questionable relationships with other women. That was the day I signed the contract that changed my life and began the eleven-year makeup/breakup cycle of our relationship. I agreed to take on the impossible mission of changing a man with my own two hands. Everything in me told me that this was all wrong, but I wanted to trust him. I wanted to have love in my life and thought that the only way I could get it was by making this man change into what I wanted him to be. After all, he did ask for my help, right?

Here's what's interesting... On one hand I trusted too much, and on the other, I didn't trust at all. I trusted Jackson wholeheartedly, while turning my nose up to my own instincts. Not only was my trust scale unbalanced, but I was putting my precious jewels in the wrong basket! I trusted him totally and didn't trust my instincts at all. I didn't trust the friends and family who loved me. I didn't trust what was right before my eyes. The trust that I claimed to have in God was also misplaced. I was trusting God to change Jackson, but would not trust that God would lead me to the right man if I would simply leave the wrong one alone. My trust capacity was all out of whack because I wanted what I wanted—a boyfriend. Because of that, I made a conscious decision to ignore all of the caution signs right from the beginning.

When you get the sense that something just isn't right, don't ignore it. Pay close attention. Ignoring it the first time can be the beginning of a devastating cycle, as you become more immune to the subtle warnings that come later. The more you ignore, the better you get at making the case for why you should stick around. The better you get at defending behavior that disrespects you. The better you get at blinding yourself to the truth of your situation. In no time you'll become a pro at flinging your heart to the flames.

The other extreme on the trust scale is paranoia. While my issue was about being more on the naïve end of the scale, I know plenty of women who are so closed, they don't trust at all. In their eyes, everyone is covertly up to no good. The dating pool is full of pee. Everyone lies, everyone cheats, and they all want nothing more than to get you in bed. These women (and men, too) take this mentality and approach the world of dating with a vengeance. They walk around with a guard so impenetrable they repel anyone who truly does have good intentions—because most of us can smell a disgruntled woman long before the first hello.

My sister, if you push your way through the world with a chip on your shoulder, you'll attract other people with chips on their shoulders. As the two of you begin to affirm each other's cynical beliefs about love, you'll grow to be convinced that your bitter take on the world is absolutely right. And, in fact, this bitter take *will* be absolutely right (for you) because what you put out to other people is exactly what you will get back. Throw out an attitude, a little lack of trust, and some bitterness into the world, and that's exactly what you'll get back. As long as you approach the world with your defenses up high, with your fists set and ready to punch something rather than to give and receive, those who are actually ready for love will do everything they can to avoid you. Take a deep breath. Relax your muscles. Unclench your fists. Trust your instincts so that you don't accidentally punch love square in the face.

It's also important to know that your instincts don't just speak up when things are about to go bad. Your instincts also lead you to what is good—that is, if you listen to them. If you've met a good person, the best way to know that this is a good person is to relax those fists, breathe, and pay attention to what your heart and your instincts are telling you. Do you feel a sense of peace? Peace is a great indicator that you're on the right track. But remember—before you can be at peace with other people, you must first be at peace with yourself. If you don't have internal peace, be sure to go back and take care of that first.

If you don't follow your instincts, you may end up following that voice that speaks out of loneliness and fear, which can either lead you down the road of over trusting the wrong person, or straight-up paranoia over anything that looks your way. Listen to your heart. It wants to protect you. It wants the best for you—even in those moments when you don't.

Love you,

Dr. Pamela

THE ART OF
RELOVING

CHAPTER EIGHT

RELOVE YOURSELF

Life is about change. Sometimes it's painful. Sometimes it's beautiful, but most of the time, it's both.

—Farrah Gray
Twitter Post, January 2, 2013

Letter 28

WAKE UP TO LOVE

My Sister,

Once you have taken the time to refocus and rebuild, you may begin to feel ready to welcome new love into your life. Stepping back into the game is not always easy. Sometimes we get so pumped to play again that we psych ourselves into believing that we're ready, when in fact, we're dreadfully out of shape. On the other extreme, we may be so terrified of being reinjured, we stay close to the sidelines. What's most ideal is that you take your time to slowly reintroduce yourself to the game—by practicing, by getting back into shape, and by developing a set of strategies.

Healing yourself is not just a cliché—it is an absolute must for anyone who wants healthy love. A wounded person seeking love is a dangerous, unappealing combination. It's dangerous for you and unappealing to the guy who ends up dealing with you. The game is not to be approached with haste, falling for the first thing that breathes. And it is not to be approached with fear, running from *anything* that breathes. Neither extreme will serve you well. One may take you into reinjury, and the other into loneliness.

After my divorce, I literally had to teach myself how to love again; not in the way I had done it before, but in a much healthier and fulfilling way. I also realized that my marriage wasn't the only unhealthy relationship in my life and that I had become an all-around guarded, unemotional person. So much so that after I left Jackson, I found that opening up to new people— no matter who they were—was painfully difficult. My way of existing around him had become my way of existing around everyone else: closed, guarded, defensive, and ready to run to protect myself. This mindset and the behaviors that followed it would never fly if I ever expected to find the love I so desired to have in my life. If I wanted to have healthy, fulfilling love in my life, I had to *be* healthy, fulfilling love. I just had no idea how. When I met Najee, I flung open the doors of my heart like a careless, hopeless romantic looking for my happily ever after. Little did I know, I had to relearn to love by first healing and loving myself. Only then would I truly understand what it meant to give and to receive and to be a vessel of love again.

I got my real wake-up call in Jamaica. Najee and I decided to take a spontaneous trip a year after I moved to Atlanta. It made perfect sense at the time. Neither of us had ever been on a cruise. We were close friends. Surely, we'd have a great time together. I was still in love with Najee, so for me, this was going to be the romantic getaway I had always dreamed of. Finally. I spent the weeks before the trip shopping for the cutest swimsuits and sexiest dresses. I was careful to schedule my nail and eyebrow appointments as close to the departure dates as possible. I bought my first pair of designer sunglasses and special ordered a dress to wear for a formal, romantic dinner overlooking the ocean. I was giddy about the thought of sailing the high seas to beautiful Jamaica with Najee. Was it just a coincidence that we were sailing away on Mother's Day weekend? Not for me! Not only was it going to be the romantic getaway of my life, but it was going to be the first time someone would make Mother's Day truly special for me. No woman on this earth was happier than I was as I anticipated this cruise of the century. And maybe...finally...we would take our friendship to a new level. This trip, without a doubt, was going to be a turning point for us.

For Najee there wasn't quite so much excitement in his preparation. It was cool that we were going to Jamaica, but he just wasn't one to get giddy over stuff like that. I remember calling him from Atlanta a couple of days before we left to ask what he was going to wear. He seemed to be annoyed by the question and responded with a dismissive, "I don't get all stressed out over stuff like that." I was taken aback by his flat lack of enthusiasm. *Really, Mr. Fashion Guy? And who the heck is stressed out? I'm going to Jamaica!* But I left it alone and assumed that perhaps I had caught him on a bad day. It was the first time I noticed a difference in our approaches to this cruise, but I did what I have always done so well. I ignored the signs and kept pushing forward.

As much as I tried to ignore the differences, I quickly learned that we were not on the same page. Still. As we crossed the beautiful blue ocean that Mother's Day weekend, I slowly came to realize what this cruise was for Najee—a chance to get away and focus on writing his music, and a chance to experience a cruise for the first time with his home girl. Not the woman of his dreams or the woman who melted his heart. No. His home girl.

Once again, our very different expectations came crashing together. As we walked around like homeboys—no hand-holding, no affection, no sweet talk—I was exploding inside. He'd leave me in the room to explore the ship without inviting me along; he wasn't interested in joining me as I waded through the crystal clear waters of the coast; and he begrudgingly humored me by dragging himself along on the nights I wanted to go out and get a feel for the cruise ship night life. I wanted to cry as we sat in silence over meals, and I fought back tears as I saw other couples standing on the deck in warm embraces. It was all I could do not to fall out into a tantrum on the middle of the ship. His mantra for the weekend was a shrug of the shoulders and a cool, "I don't care" to nearly everything I suggested. Karaoke, dancing, massages, the Limbo. It was like being escorted by a member of the British army. No excitement, no emotion...just incredibly heartbreaking.

The last day of the cruise was Mother's Day. It was not quite as special as I had imagined it would be. Najee never wished me a happy Mother's Day, offered no gift, and never even mentioned the day to me. Yet, he demonstrated in a few ways that he was fully aware of what day it was. When we were out shopping on the island, for example, I pointed out a dress that I absolutely loved. When I wandered away to another store, I looked back and saw him point that very dress out to the sales lady, and he proceeded to purchase it. I screamed like a teenager inside. *He's buying me the dress!* I later learned that he didn't purchase the dress for me, as I had immediately assumed, but for his son's mother as a Mother's Day gift. Crushing. I also stood next to him as he expressed a heartfelt "Happy Mother's Day" to an older woman we came across whom he later explained reminded him of an old wise aunt. Was I even there? Did I exist? His message couldn't have been louder or clearer. This was not our romantic getaway, and I was still exactly who he always said I was—his home girl (you know...kind of like one of his boys).

As we parted ways and loaded up our separate cabs, it took everything in me to choke back the fountain of tears that had accumulated over the course of the weekend. I managed to keep it cool—that is, until he was out of my view. It's not like me to cry publicly, but as I sat there alone in the back seat of my cab, the tears wouldn't stop. I tried to remain silent, but my body jerked uncontrollably like it did when I cried as a child. I felt like such a fool. The cab driver seemed to notice. He didn't ask for an explanation, but told me the story of how he met his wife and how he loved her more than anything in the world. He told me how beautiful she was and how much he missed her when he had to go to work. She was his whole world, he told me. How I wished to be loved so deeply by someone. *Why has no one loved me in this way? How is it that I was once married and never experienced this kind of love?*

Then, as if he could hear my thoughts, he said something I will never forget in his deep Cuban accent, "And you too, Pamela, will have someone who loves you that way. Don't let anyone give you less than what you deserve. You are a beautiful girl and someone is going to love you. He doesn't deserve you."

And that was it. I had told him nothing about my weekend and how deeply my heart had been broken. He heard my story through the sobbing I tried to hide, and this cab driver couldn't help himself. He was my angel that day. He stopped me in my tracks with his words. I was so heartbroken that I couldn't stop crying, but amazingly, God kept sending random people my way who felt compelled to impart some uplifting words throughout the entire day. "You're beautiful," one older man uttered to me as I passed him in the airport. "God bless you," said an elderly woman to me on the plane. I was devastated, but I embraced the words of that cab driver and those other angels. Someone was going to love me the way that man loved his wife. My task was to get over Najee and get ready to receive that love. Refocus, rebuild, and relove. I did all three over the course of that summer and fall. By winter, I was ready for love and didn't even realize it.

This final section, my sister, is about being open to loving again, and about loving as a new and improved you. Heartbreak hurts. But think of it this way—it may have been exactly what you needed to get past where you were and to get to where you're going. I'll tell you this much, if I had not finally opened up my eyes and let go of Najee when I did, I'd probably still be sitting around, hoping, praying, and begging for him to be my man. Lord, I am so glad I'm not there anymore! If I had known what was waiting right around the corner for me, I would've let go a long time ago! I will echo for you the words of my guardian angel and lovesick cab driver: "And you too, my sister, will have someone who loves you the way that he loves his wife. Don't let anyone give you less than what you deserve. You are a beautiful girl, and someone is going to love you." Your job, my friend, is to get ready!

Reloving is the process of stepping back into the realm of love after heartbreak. It requires that you shed the crippling fear, bitterness, doubt, and anger that can hinder love from flourishing in your life. This is why refocusing and rebuilding are both so vitally important before reloving. When you relove, you give yourself permission to open up and love again in a healthy way—not out of desperation or with hopes that someone will love you back, and not under circumstances that compromise your dignity and personal safety, but with a joy that comes from mutual respect, understanding, and true love. This is loving with a new purpose.

A healthy love is one in which you are emotionally, mentally, and spiritually at peace with yourself and the person you are with. *Emotionally*, you are stable. You're no longer on an emotional roller coaster—up one minute and in pieces the next. *Mentally*, your thoughts are clear. You are confident in your ability to make sound decisions because you've taken the time to learn from the experiences of your past. You trust yourself. *Spiritually*, you have a positive outlook on life, and you fully believe in the possibility of experiencing the love that you deserve. You are able to see beyond the circumstances of today and appreciate the greater purpose in all things. Being at peace spiritually allows you to fully appreciate where you are today and enables you to use today to prepare for all that is to come.

When welcoming love into your life, there are three small tasks that you'll want to accomplish: rediscover love for yourself, reconnect with those who love you, and learn how to love and forgive the one who hurt you. The next four letters will focus on how to relove *yourself.* Get your highlighter out, take notes, and prepare to give yourself all the attention you deserve.

Love,

Dr. Pamela

Letter 29

Healing Wounds

My Sister,

I'm not usually one to get worked up over what goes on with celebrities and their love lives, but lately, there has just been so much to notice—so many unhealthy situations to observe and learn from. Maybe it's just my heightened sense of awareness as a single woman, but I see these same unhealthy patterns playing out in the lives of not-so-famous people. It has become a classic theme of entertainment news: the handsome new beau on the arm of the beautiful actress who just ended her third marriage two months prior. All of this bliss with no thought to the type of healing that might need to take place after the ripping apart of a recent breakup.

All too often, our lives reflect the patterns of these glamorous celebrities. We seek immediate comfort from the pain by resting in the arms of someone else—anyone else—as soon as possible. I know this, because I'm just as guilty as anyone else. I've been there. This was the critical mistake I made with Najee. He was comforting. He helped me forget about the pain. He was my escape from reality. I fooled myself into believing that new love—as quickly as possible—would heal the wounds of old love. Najee's friendship did help me heal in many ways, but the emotion associated with falling in love with him did not. Back to back heartbreaks—first with Jackson, and then with Najee—taught me how important it is to step back and give myself some time to get it together before moving on to the next thing.

I understand why we do it. Finding new love or even a new fling as quickly as possible keeps our minds off the enormity of what has just happened in our lives. It allows us to bask in the glory of feeling loved again (even if that love is just a fantasy). It also gives us that secret satisfaction of revenge as we appear to have moved on with our lives. Best of all (and this really is the best part), it keeps us from having to actually face those demons we keep kicking back into the closet.

What's missing here? Taking your mind off of what has happened, hiding behind affection, basking in revenge, and living in denial all circumvent the healing process. Perhaps it's worth considering that seeking immediate comfort should not be top priority after a breakup. Perhaps it's best to allow yourself to *feel* the discomfort. When the primary objective is to feel better and not to actually heal, we tend to seek comfort by any means necessary. We numb ourselves—through over drinking, over working, over sexing, or handing our hearts over to the next contestant. Dangerous move, sister!

Of course we all want comfort. We want to feel better. But after heartbreak, comfort is a luxury we have to work to secure. That work doesn't usually happen overnight. Sometimes, living outside the comfort zone is exactly the challenge we need to force us to look at ourselves and change what needs to be changed. It doesn't matter who was to blame for the breakup—whether you cheated or were cheated on, or regardless of who squandered whose money away. Odds are, you have some self-assessing to do before stepping into another situation.

Unfortunately, many of us flat-out refuse to spend the necessary time with ourselves to get to a place of true peace before moving on. Why is that? Do we dislike ourselves? Are we afraid to stare at ourselves in the face? I know that the thought of going from long-term relationship to single lady can be a scary one, but it can also be quite liberating and life-changing. It's all in how you approach it. The status of "single" can give us the time and space we need to prepare for the love and the life we truly deserve. Running to the first person who agrees to open the door will not.

Navigate Your Own Ship

When guided by a fear of being alone, many of us become like stowaways, hiding out on the ships of strangers, walking around with fake expressions of strength, as if we're entitled to be there. We hover around the buffet tables and sleep in vacant cabins, making ourselves at home because we've never made a home for ourselves. We fool ourselves into believing that we are being taken care of, when really, we are slowly losing a sense of dignity and internal security. We think we're in control, but have turned all control over to the captain of those ships who have provided us a false sense of refuge. What a crippling way to exist in the world!

When your ship has been destroyed, you may need to spend some uncomfortable time in the water strengthening your muscles, learning how to swim better, how to sense the danger of sharks, how to overcome fears. The last thing you need to do is find another captain to depend on. The truth is, you just don't know your own strength until you've taken on the waters of the high seas alone. When you've mastered the challenge, the fear, and the solitude, you will eventually learn to navigate your own ship. You will learn how to navigate your life. You'll find that you can make it to dry land on your own, where you can begin to build up your empire. This is independence at its finest, girlfriend. This means having your own set of know-how tools, your own strength, your own sense of control. Navigating your own ship is just irresistibly sexy!

Before you can truly realize your strength, you've got to build yourself up and develop some faith in your ability to survive on your own. You can't get there by jumping from one captain's ship to another. This strategy only teaches you survival. It fails to take you to the next level—the level of optimal living, of building your own home and erecting your own empire of stability. After heartbreak, we are already in a weak state of mind. When we take that state of mind into another situation without healing wounds or addressing unhealthy patterns of behavior (like settling for someone who doesn't meet our needs) we never operate above survival mode and further continue the cycle of jumping from ship to ship.

If you want the next relationship to be a better one—a healthy one—it is essential to take some time to heal and strengthen yourself. This process is supposed to make you better. It is supposed to develop you into an even more amazing person, to take you to a new and higher level of living. Push through the pain and the loneliness to find your strength. If you don't give yourself the time, that baggage will just continue to chase you from relationship to relationship, and it won't go away until you finally turn around to face them once and for all.

The goal: next time you run into potential love, you'll want to be able to say, "Hey, I've spent time building this empire of mine. What do you have to bring to the table?" And if they are able to present you with an empire of their own (which can show up in many forms), well, you just might have something there. This is what you want to shoot for—not two empty souls crashing together, but two well-grounded empires that unite. Take the time you need to build up that empire of yours, so that

no matter what your status is (single or in a relationship), you
have something to stand on with confidence and pride.

Love,

Dr. Pamela

Letter 30

TAKE CARE OF YOUR BODY

My Sister,

One of the most important ways to love yourself is by taking care of that body that you live in. This means on the inside and on the outside. Caring for your body entails everything from eating right and exercising regularly to jazzing yourself up so you feel great about what you see in the mirror, even if you're not going anywhere. As superficial as this may sound, looking and feeling good truly are important aspects of caring for yourself.

This is one of the areas of improvement I get most excited about because it comes with rewards that I get to enjoy each time I look in the mirror. I had never felt younger, sexier, and more confident in myself than I felt after I left Jackson. I was a breath of fresh air *to myself.* This glowing confidence has drawn some of the most amazing people into my life—people who also have a glowing confidence of their own. To get to this place, I focused on three very important aspects of my physical health: stress management, regular exercise, and healthy eating habits. Collectively, adopting new habits in these three areas resulted in my new carefree spirit, my ability to flaunt it in jeans that were four sizes smaller, and a greater level of energy to tackle my goals in life.

Work It Out

When I first started my workout routine, I didn't set out to do anything revolutionary. I just knew that I needed to adopt a healthier lifestyle that would keep me from succumbing to poor health as a result of stress and low energy. My stress level was high, and each time I allowed myself to bask and wallow in that stress, I felt the physical ramifications. The arthritis that ran through my genes started to plague my young body, I gradually gained weight, and my digestive system began to rebel against me. I needed to execute a plan to keep this stress at bay and keep my body from falling apart, so I exercised. I didn't exercise with the goal of losing weight. I wasn't trying to become a body builder or a health guru. My goal was simple—to get my happy endorphins going and to eliminate the debilitating effects of stress. And it worked. On my worst days, I found that after a workout—at even the most moderate level—I felt energized, refreshed, and relieved. No matter what I actually looked like, I felt sexy leaving the gym, and I noticed that I even began to walk as if I knew I was the sexiest thing to cross an intersection.

I started on the treadmill. My intention was not to do anything difficult—just a comfortable twenty-minute walk. That was it. A whopping seventy calories, and I thought I was doing it big! But you know what? I *was*. I had no idea that I was laying the foundation for a whole new lifestyle. Every day, I went into the gym, got on that treadmill, and did my little walk. Accomplishing that on a daily basis made me feel victorious. Who knew that only months later, I would be on that same treadmill doing an intense, fat-melting one-hour sprint/powerwalk workout? I was all about establishing a new routine, a new habit, and a new lifestyle. It wasn't long before my body began to crave more. I went from walking to challenging myself to run for sixty seconds at a time. I went from twenty-minute workouts to thirty-minute workouts. I didn't run myself into the ground. I responded to the "more" my body was asking for. When you treat your body well, it wants more. But you have to get started first.

It probably took about a good month or two before I lost a pound because it wasn't about losing weight. I needed the stress relief and was grateful when those awful stress symptoms began to fade. Actually, I thank God that I wasn't trying to lose weight because the stagnant scale would have stressed me out, and that would have been counterproductive. If you do want to lose weight, don't let my slow start discourage you—the weight loss came in a very healthy way as I continued to increase the intensity of my workouts and as I learned how to eat the right foods. It was all very much a learning process. I recommend first focusing on establishing a healthy routine, and once you've got a rhythm going, then set some realistic weight-loss goals.

Within six months, working out daily became a regular part of my life routine. As I became more committed to a healthier lifestyle, I began to do more reading and research on diet and exercise to be sure I was doing it correctly. I couldn't afford to hire a personal trainer or a nutritionist, so I educated myself. I learned to pay attention to calories, to eat greens and protein-rich foods, and to avoid fast food altogether. The exercise alone helped to curb cravings for my ultimate weakness—candy. I was a certified candy fiend. It became my drug of choice when I was stressed out. Yet, miraculously, when I was on a steady workout routine, my body didn't crave candy at all. I also made simple substitutions like drinking nonfat milk instead of low-fat milk and zero-calorie sports drinks instead of full containers of my beloved cranberry cherry juice. As an adult who never really grew out of the childhood "I don't like vegetables" mentality, I managed to develop a love for *some* veggies like spinach, sweet potatoes, broccoli, tomatoes, and bell peppers. For those veggies I didn't like to eat, I learned to puree those and cook them into foods like eggs, rice, pastas, and even desserts. I keep a stash of pureed veggies in the freezer to this day and cook them into almost every meal I prepare. My philosophy about eating right and working out is that it shouldn't be terribly painful. It should be enjoyable. I was patient with myself through the process and used creative ways to eat better foods while also continuing workouts in the gym.

I'm certainly no certified health expert, but between my self-education, the exercising, and the better food choices, I managed to get myself into great shape. I became my own expert—an expert at getting Pamela right. I highly recommend that you do some research and craft a strategy than can work for you. If getting in shape is a new endeavor for you, start by making it a goal to develop a healthy routine. If you develop the routine and stay away from the scale, the weight loss will come. Just focus first and foremost on living healthy.

Adorn the Skin You're In

When you pass by a mirror, do you pause and gaze upon the beauty staring back at you, or do you hurry by to avoid facing yourself? Eating right and exercising keep us alive and well, but looking nice helps to keep the head held high. How well do you take care of yourself on the outside? It's hard to feel great about yourself if you never do anything to make yourself look and feel sexy, beautiful, gorgeous, and amazing. I'm not talking about trying to keep up with society's standard of beauty. I'm talking about establishing your own standard of beauty. This can mean keeping up with your hair, throwing on a little makeup from time to time, keeping your nails manicured, or whatever it takes for you to feel great in your skin. Try not to settle for walking around in a night scarf and house shoes all day. Don't embody a depressed, woe-is-me persona. A great way to lift your spirits and to overcome feeling like a hot mess is to avoid *looking* like a hot mess. I'm not suggesting that you plaster on the fake eyelashes and glittering makeup each time you leave the house. In fact, many women like myself actually prefer not to wear makeup. That is absolutely okay! Just find a happy medium that you can be proud of—one that makes you want to spend a few extra seconds admiring that dazzling reflection staring back at you in the mirror.

I credit much of my outer transformation to Najee. He's a classy guy with a unique, attractive eye for fashion. This man easily stands out in any crowd. Bright colors, flashy hats, argyle socks, and bowties—this was the guy who introduced me to fashion, who took me to a department store and helped me pick out my first stylish pair of name-brand heels. As a thirty-three-year-old woman, I had never spent more than thirty dollars on a pair of shoes. Never in my wildest dreams did it occur to me that shoes would ever matter. I was that chick in the office with the splitting worn heel so severe that people could hear the exposed metal bottom *clip clopping* against the floor from a mile away. For me, fashion had always been generic. It was whatever matching combination of blacks and grays I could pull together on a dime. Najee opened my eyes to a whole new world. After that first pair of designer heels, I was hooked. I spent the next year building up my wardrobe, little by little, replacing my loafers with mostly reasonably priced flashy heels (some, not so reasonably priced), and my blacks and grays with bright, bold colors. The timing was perfect. I had my new sexy body, I was changing cities and careers, and because I was loving my new look, I was able to hold my head up high while inhaling the many compliments I received for each great new pair of heels I flaunted. Najee gave me great eye-opening tips, and I followed like an eager music student taking lessons from Bach.

Treat Yourself Like a Queen

My single lady era was also the time in my life when I learned how to pamper myself. This was great stress relief and became a great priority for me. I made it a point to get a massage at least once a month, and I got a manicure and pedicure every few weeks. It wasn't always within my budget to treat myself, but I made it a priority. When I could afford to do it, I did it, or I would find other creative ways of sneaking relaxation in—like getting a ten-dollar chair massage in the mall or finding an online coupon for a massage discount. This very important pamper-me time kept me calm and at peace with my life. It helped me slow down. Everything I was doing gradually developed into a lifestyle of balance. I was eating better, exercising regularly, getting relaxing massages, and putting in the effort to look as nice as I could. It wasn't long before I literally had to replace most of my wardrobe with clothes that fit my new body and embrace a new schedule to accommodate my self-loving lifestyle.

If you are not already maintaining healthy eating habits, exercising, and reducing stress, the time to start is now. If you're walking around looking like a brokenhearted hot mess, transform yourself into someone who can hold her head up high. It's your body, and it's your responsibility alone to take care of it. When you love yourself, you take care of your body, and when you take care of your body, you love yourself even more. See the cycle? Start small. If you stick with the smaller goals long enough, your effort will create a snowball effect that can change your entire life routine for the better.

Remember, this is not about looking good on the outside to attract a new man. It is about saving yourself, preserving yourself for the long run, and planting very important seeds for loving yourself. Loving what you see when you look in the mirror is a great reward for taking care of yourself. If you get stuck in any of these areas, don't hesitate to ask for help from a personal trainer, a life coach, a health expert, or even a friend. This is your life. Take your health and well being seriously. You'll love yourself for it.

Love,

Dr. Pamela

Letter 31

BECOMING BEAUTIFUL

My Sister,

When you look in the mirror, are you happy with what you see? Do you see your beauty? Do you feel beautiful on the inside? Much of what I talked about in the previous letter will help you feel better about yourself. But truly seeing yourself as beautiful doesn't happen overnight, especially if this is something you struggle with personally. Internalizing a true sense of beauty includes a combination of what you physically do for yourself, the people you surround yourself with, and the messages that you take in on a regular basis.

While Jackson and I were only married for five years, we were involved with each other for nearly twelve. Before him, there was the year and a half with Brian. Neither of these guys was very big on compliments. Brian struggled so much with his own identity and self worth that it wasn't in him to pay a compliment or offer words of encouragement to anyone. According to Brian, I was always the liar (surely our son wasn't really his), the one who hurt him (hence, the numerous suicide threats), and the one who thoroughly complicated his life (now he had a child to be responsible for). Although I knew none of this was true about me, it affected the way I saw myself nonetheless.

Jackson lived with his protective shell up at all times. He was too cool to pay a compliment. "Beautiful is a word that just isn't even a part of my vocabulary," he once told me. How very sad on a number of levels. In my opinion, beautiful—or at least a synonym of the word—should be a part of everyone's vocabulary. Without it, how does one acknowledge what is beautiful about life? How could you look at a sunset and not think about how beautiful it is? How could you see the changing leaves of fall and not think beauty? How could you stand at the edge of the ocean and not find beauty in its dance with the sky? And how could you wake up next to your wife every morning and not see beauty in her? "Yeah, you cool" will only fly for so long. I wanted Jackson to let his guard down and call it like he saw it. I wasn't just cool. I was beautiful, dammit! If words like beautiful, amazing, awesome, great, and wonderful are not a part of your vocabulary, you are not enjoying or appreciating life enough.

I once saw a Twitter post written by Mastin Kipp of The Daily Love that said, "If you are too cool to love, your heart will freeze to death. Express yo' love." Jackson was too cool to love. So cool that he didn't know how to express himself. Perhaps, he did see beauty in life or in his wife, but if beauty was what he saw, he sure wasn't able to express it beyond uttering a nonchalant, "Yeah, that's cool." If I couldn't express the beauty or awesomeness of life that I see every day, I'd implode.

This lack of expression is what I subjected myself to for more than a decade. Two men who were too cool or too messed up to ever say that I was beautiful, that I looked nice, that they loved my smile, that I was talented, that I had a sweet spirit. I was all of these things, but I never heard it from them. I'm not saying that it was Brian's and Jackson's responsibility to make me feel beautiful and to help me see beauty in myself. It was my responsibility to ensure that I surrounded myself with people who would be willing to affirm (rather than downplay) my greatest qualities, and who at a bare minimum would not consistently put me down.

Who and what I invited and allowed to stay in my life were totally my responsibility. By the time I was finished with these guys, my self-image was so distorted, I would fall into a complete state of shock when I received compliments from a stranger. When I became single, I often heard, *you are so fine... wow, you're beautiful...* or *your hair is gorgeous.* At first, I didn't know how to respond. I couldn't believe that they were talking to *me* and that they were serious. I was so used to not receiving compliments from Brian or Jackson that I didn't know what to do when I started hearing them. The more I took care of myself and carried myself with confidence, the more the compliments came. The happier I became, the more people seemed to be drawn to me. My happiness alone seemed to translate into greater and greater levels of beauty.

RECLAIM BEAUTY

Spending a decade of my life with a guy who couldn't bring his mouth to utter the word "beautiful" certainly affected the way I viewed myself. When I left him, I had to be proactive about rediscovering my own beauty. I surrounded myself with people who saw and acknowledged my strength and beauty. I discovered what it actually meant to be beautiful—that it wasn't just about the way I looked, but it was totally about who I was. I focused on the areas of my life in which beauty existed. It didn't matter how often I heard it from other people. If I didn't see it and believe it for myself, I could not embrace my beauty. I would have a hard time holding my head up high to exude the confidence that would help me live out my purpose and to attract the type of love that I had always desired.

I made it a point to reclaim my beauty. I exercised, changed my wardrobe, and took care of my outer appearance. To reinforce belief in my own beauty, I soaked in all of the compliments I received for my new look—the sassy shoes, the jeans that complemented my shape, and the creative, sexy hairstyles I was donning. I made it a point to compliment myself—to say out loud that I looked beautiful or sexy so that I would get used to hearing those words in my next relationship. I focused on those things I loved to do. I treated other people with love and respect. Doing these things made me feel good about myself. I complimented people who touched me with their kindness, friendship, or even their nice shoes. What I found was that feeling beautiful translated to carrying myself like a beautiful woman, and it was this way of carrying myself that attracted people to me.

Put sexy and beautiful on your agenda. But strike a reasonable balance. Don't become self-serving, vain, or obnoxious with it. But don't walk around hating yourself, either. As you begin to feel better about yourself, others will also notice your beauty and confidence. Reclaim your beauty and wear it proudly. Don't rely on others to do that for you. Start your own campaign. Your beauty is your own. No one can flaunt your stuff like you can!

Love,

Dr. Pamela

Letter 32

DANCE MORE

My Sister,

One of the first things I did after leaving Jackson was dance in the empty, unfurnished living room of my new apartment the day I signed my lease. I danced to release the tension I had held on to for so many years. I danced to praise God for a second chance at life. I danced to celebrate a strength that I didn't know I had. I didn't need music. I didn't need a dance floor. All I needed was a grateful heart, a joyful spirit, and a little hope for my new, unknown future. Little did I know, that brief episode of dancing in my living room was the beginning of a new era of celebration in my life. The fact that my family was now in pieces was devastating. Finally facing the truth about my marriage was crushing. But I knew that if I dwelled on the fear and the pain, I would stay broken. I needed a new approach that would keep me uplifted and full of life. With each small victory, I made it a point to dance and celebrate my progress. I learned to look at my challenges differently—as opportunities for victory.

The week I left Jackson just happened to be the same week I taught my very first graduate-level course. I was a newly minted Ph.D., and our department chair decided to take a chance on me by allowing me to teach some graduate and doctoral courses. I was thrilled for the opportunity. I had been hounding him about considering me for any job opportunities for nearly a year, and I was finally getting my chance. When I walked into that classroom—internally broken to pieces—I already had three strikes against me: I was, by far, the youngest person in the room, I was the only African American female professor in the department, and I was just about as new and inexperienced as they come. It was hard enough to wade through *those* challenges, but to add to that, I also carried with me the weight of that week's baggage on my shoulders. As hard as I tried to walk in with a smile, shake off the fear, and prove that I had what it took to be there, my internal angst somehow showed.

Class that night was a disaster. I was teaching leadership from a million miles away. It was the worst teaching night of my life. There was no escaping the front of that classroom. I had to perform. I'm not exactly sure what it was that the students saw, but several of them complained to another faculty member that night about how disheveled I appeared to be. There were mistakes on the syllabus. I didn't explain the assignments clearly. My lecture was all over the place. Fortunately, my colleague was fully aware of what was going on in my personal life and urged me not to get discouraged.

In spite of the disaster I knew I had orchestrated that night, what do you think I did when I got home? I marched into my living room and I danced like I was center stage on Broadway. I danced! What a relief to finally exhale within the safe walls of my empty little apartment. That night marked the beginning of a new era in my life.

I taught myself how to dance and rejoice through hardship so that my challenges could never find a way to defeat me. There truly is victory for your praise. When you dance, you learn to dance away any sense of defeat that tries to creep in. And if you've been defeated—as I felt I had been on that first night of class—you learn to dance *through* that defeat, which totally confuses the part of you that wants to wallow in self-pity. There's no room for self-pity when you're dancing. The two cannot exist in the same space. Even if the dancing brings tears to your eyes, and even if you have to scream out the pain, you're still dancing, and you're still moving yourself closer to healing. So, dance through that pain.

It wasn't long before dancing just became a way of life. Once I mastered dancing through my pain, I began dancing through each little victory. When I finished a workout, for example, I celebrated with a quick victory dance. When I was offered a full-time faculty position in Atlanta a year later, I danced and screamed in my car. When I was approved to purchase and build a new home for me and the kids a year after that, I danced each time I walked through the piles of concrete, wood, and dirt as the house was being constructed.

Dancing became so important to me because over the years, I had become utterly numb to life. I had to teach myself how to live again. I had somehow managed to attach myself to men who didn't know what it meant to celebrate life. Brian, especially. In the year and a half he and I were together, he forgot my birthday twice. In fact, he broke up with me on my birthday in our first year when I was pregnant. And then there was Jackson, who lived behind a wall that kept him subdued at all times. If ever I jumped for joy over anything, he'd give me a disapproving look to indicate that I needed to calm down. Even Najee abhorred holidays like Christmas and Valentine's Day because of "our society's obsession with commercialization." *Oh, lighten up already! I just want to celebrate something!* But over the years, I gradually abandoned my celebratory nature and retreated to an imprisoned life of utter numbness.

When I learned to dance, I slowly evolved from that state of numbness, silence, and passivity, into a person who found her voice. I finally let down the guard that forced me to plaster on a fake smile and downplay those things that brought me joy. I learned how to smile for real. I learned how to rejoice—truly rejoice—for all that was happening in my life. When I began to dance more, my whole outlook on life changed. For the first time in more than a decade, I was filled with hope for a great future.

This is the kind of mindset that brings positive people and experiences into our lives. This is not just fairytale stuff, girlfriend. This is how life works. When you let your inhibitions go and allow yourself to rejoice in the good and the bad and simply dance, life becomes more enjoyable to live. I dare you to give it a shot. What will you dance about today? Pull down those shades, kick off your shoes, and give it a try!

Learning to Love Your Life

Dancing is not just about jumping around and moving those hips, but that surely is a start. Once you've got that basic idea down, you can begin transforming your life into one that is *accustomed* to joy. Here's the key—get your life to the point where being happy, joyful, and fulfilled is your new normal. Get to the point where you are used to smiling and laughing till your belly hurts and to where you are thoroughly at peace as a single woman. Experience true peace. This is crucial because once you get there, anyone who steps into your life and disrupts that peace will immediately rub you the wrong way. You'll notice it, and they won't be welcome to stay. It is much easier to recognize a buzz kill when you are in a good place in your life than when you are already at a low point.

If you hate your life and you hate yourself and you live miserably each day, when you meet another miserable being, the two of you will think you're living in perfect harmony—and you probably will be! But that kind of harmony doesn't exactly end with happily ever after. While you're single and before you get involved with someone else, get to happy first. Live and breathe and walk in *happy* so that anyone who steps into your life has to prove themselves a worthy addition—that what they have to offer you is added joy and not pain. They have to prove that they are not there to disrupt your peace of mind and renewed joy for life. Find your happy place and let no one intrude on that.

I'm not asking that you give each and every person you meet the side eye and assume that they're up to no good. I am asking that you first find your peace and happiness and then guard it at all costs. I am asking that you take the same precautions that a bear would take to protect her cubs. She's not welcoming any stranger into her den until she knows that this stranger is bringing the goods to her household. In that same sense, protect your babies—peace and happiness—by making sure that anyone you welcome in brings you and your babies the goods. If not, they've got to go. Plain and simple.

My newly developed love for dancing and finding joy in my life began with Najee but didn't really kick in until after I let him go. I spent so much time and energy trying to match his level of cool to impress him that I had forgotten how to dance...once again. I was back where I was when I was married to Jackson—walking on eggshells. I hadn't given myself time to get to a place of real joy before I fell for Najee, so I managed to fool myself (again) into believing that what we had was something I had always wanted. He was a great friend who made me laugh, but ultimately, our very different sets of wants and needs clashed. I wanted lovey-dovey, teenage-like romantic love. He wanted to be my homeboy. With stars in my eyes, I eventually lost sight of what peace and joy looked like because I never gave myself a chance to really experience it. I fooled myself into believing that our friendship, complete with its mismatched motives and expectations, was the peace and joy I had been seeking. I thought I if I could just stick around long enough, he would eventually love me the way I wanted to be loved. Eventually, he would reach out to hold my hand or wrap his arms around me or kiss my face and tell me how much he loves me. *If I could just stick around long enough, he'll fall in love with me.*

Sound familiar? This is exactly what I did with Jackson. *If I love him enough, he'll love me like he loves the women in his family.* I had fallen right back into my old patterns of fear and insecurity—fear of being alone and insecure about my ability to attract someone who was better for me. This fear and insecurity drove me to believe that I needed to make things happen on my own. Same mentality, same motive, different guy. It had to stop.

Najee and I reached a breaking point after that fateful Jamaican cruise. It was bound to happen because we had been headed in that direction for a long time. I wanted commitment. He wanted freedom. He had always called it a timing issue, and then it became a distance issue, so my rationale was to wait. But in my waiting, my words and actions were all relationship-oriented. I wanted to hold hands. I wanted to do weekend getaways together. I wanted him to tell me he loved me. Meanwhile, his words and actions were in no way relationship-oriented. Because I didn't know what real peace and joy felt like, I thought this was it, even as our friendship suffered more and more as time went on.

Love Yourself Like You Want to Be Loved

After the Jamaican cruise, Najee and I debriefed. He told me that I had pushed him away. Totally shocked and hurt, a light finally went on in me and I woke up. I realized what I was doing. This was Jackson all over again. I was just going to *make* this man settle down with me. It was insane. Through that conversation, I cried some hard and painful tears, and finally accepted his words and where he was. After that, I made a commitment to myself that I followed through with and never looked back. I found my happy. I decided to take deliberate action to make my life one that I loved to live. I harbored no ill feelings toward Najee. He had been honest with me from beginning to end. I thought I had been honest as well, but when I really evaluated myself, it was clear that I had actually twisted everything to look like what I wanted rather than what was. I had to move on, and that is exactly what I did.

For the first time in a decade, I made it a point to celebrate my birthday that year, rather than to sit around and hope that someone would make it special for me. I set up a night of dinner, comedy, and dancing and invited my closest girlfriends. It was the best birthday I ever had. I decided to enjoy my life on purpose by doing things I had never done before. I entered a dating challenge—a crazy, but life-changing experience I will tell you more about in Letter 38. I also spoiled the heck out of myself with dinners at my favorite restaurants, massages, and mani-pedis. By no means was I rolling in the dough, but I set a budget and made it happen—with virtual promotions and any special deals I could find. I basically dated myself and treated myself exactly how I would want a significant other to love and treat me. I took myself to church, wrote letters to myself, bought myself clothes that made me look amazing, took myself to the gym, read books about love, and cooked dinners at home that I enjoyed with a good glass of wine. I really lived it up. I genuinely grew to love myself and my life. It was at that point I recall verbally expressing to a friend, "You know—I really love being single! For the first time in my life, I am so happy!"

This is when I began to meet men who wanted exactly what I wanted out of life. I wasn't looking for it—but somehow my love for life was irresistibly contagious. For the first time in a very long time, I was the one who was sought after. I didn't have to beg someone to hold my hand. My options were endless. When I learned as a single woman what love, joy, and peace were supposed to feel like, it was not at all difficult to recognize it when I saw it. And the most interesting part? My self-love seemed to serve as a personal shield. During this phase of my life, I honestly don't recall being approached by anyone with obviously foul intentions. I seemed to attract only people who also loved their lives and wanted another life-loving person to share themselves with. What an eye-opening shift in my world! *Najee who? Jackson who?* I was worlds away from my old "please be with me" mindset.

My advice to you, my sister, is to learn to dance more. Find your happiness and be filled with joy before you bring someone else in.

Love, joy, and peace to you,

Dr. Pamela

CHAPTER NINE

RELOVE OTHERS

Sometimes finding peace means winning those inner battles.
Other times it means surrendering. The power is in knowing the
difference.

Pamela A. Larde
Twitter Post, December 28, 2011

Letter 33

LOOK AROUND...LOVE IS THERE

My Sister,

In the midst of being brokenhearted, there came a point when I was so consumed with missing Najee and licking my wounds that I almost forgot that he and I weren't the only two people left in the world. At that time, my world was all about me, me, me and how hurt I was—and it was all about him, him, him and how much I missed him. I had an amazing team of support at my side to get me out of the house and to listen when I wanted to obsess, but I was so self-absorbed that I forgot to love my family and friends the way that they so intentionally been loving me.

For many years, my life was all about survival of the heart—trying to stay strong as a young single mom after enduring the emotional roller coaster ride with Brian; desperately working to hold together a marriage that was doomed long before Jackson and I ever walked down the aisle; and holding on to the oasis that I thought I had found in Najee as if I was holding on to dear life. Between these near back-to-back situations, which collectively consumed about fifteen years of my life, my friends and loved ones did their very best to hold on with two hands as my life went through loops and senseless leaps into fire. Some hung in there. Others gave me the peace sign and never looked back. It is certainly part of the natural flow of life to have friends come and go, but at some point, I had to pull my head out of the sand and recognize who was in my corner. I had to make the effort to love them as they had been loving me. So I loved them by showing my appreciation. I loved them by being mindful of what I was sucking out of them. I loved them by asking about their lives for a change.

In my next set of letters, I'll cover how you can begin to love other people the way you want to be loved, how to rekindle old friendships that are worth saving, and what it means to reintroduce new potential for love in your life through dating. It's all about learning to love again by practicing with those "others" in your life who used to be at the forefront—your brother, a parent, even an old best friend. Those people who have loved you all along would appreciate a little attention from you. These are the people you want to practice on as you learn to love again. Entrusting your love to others may not be easy at first, but a person who is not fully able to love cannot be fully healed. In the next set of letters, I'll show you how to pursue your healing by practicing love.

Love,

Dr. Pamela

Letter 34

THE ART OF PRACTICING LOVE

My Sister,

When I think of the people who have loved me the most throughout the course of my life, I think of my mom and dad. I think of my brother who I wrestled with as a kid. I think of close female friends I've had through different phases of my life, and two of my best male friends in high school who were like big brothers to me. I even think of Najee, who reminded me that I can have a man in my life who genuinely listens to me. These people took great measures to show me that I can count on them, that they believed in me, and that our relationship was a priority. I felt secure in their presence and was blessed to have them in my life when I needed them most.

Each time I think about all that they added to my life, I consider the ways in which I touch the lives of the people who depend on me. *Can my loved ones truly count on me? Do I believe in the people I love? Do I make my relationships with family and friends a priority?* Sadly, my answers to these questions were a solid "no" for many years. It's a wonder that I had any friends at all after that long period of self-absorption and numbness. Sometimes, self-absorption is necessary for survival. For me, it was absolutely necessary as I dug in my heels and got that PhD done while juggling a full-time job, two kids, a tight budget, and a shaky marriage. I needed to stay focused to keep all of the balls of my life in the air. If I dropped one of them, there was no one other than myself who would need to go back and pick up the pieces.

I missed a lot of important events during this time period—weddings, funerals, baby showers, births, and graduations. My finances wouldn't enable me to travel. My educational pursuits kept me from spending extended amounts of time on the phone or hanging out with friends, and my shaky marriage doused any spark of zeal for life that I had once possessed. I lived that seven-year period of my life—I call it my seven-year tribulation period—as if it was all an out-of-body experience. I was in survival mode, yet dead to myself and oblivious to what was going on in the worlds of the people around me. I lived to survive. I just wanted to get through it all.

Once I finally did make it through and out into the light, I realized that I needed to bring some love back into my life. I had pushed some relationships to the wayside, and the one I had just ended was not at all a healthy one. I needed to learn again what it meant to express love to those who were important to me. I needed to practice expressing love within the context of a healthy relationship. My training ground became those people in my life who already loved me and managed to stick around.

Perhaps you've done a better job of nurturing those important relationships. If that's the case, I commend you for that. It's not always an easy thing to do, depending on how the dynamics of your past relationships affected your life. When I go through difficult times, I tend to disappear. I avoid people and sink into my own little world, determined to take care of the problem myself while faking happy until I emerge either totally beaten up or victorious. I know other people who do the exact opposite. They rely almost entirely on their friends and family as sounding boards, punching bags, or shoulders to cry on—so much so, the family and friends begin to dash out of dodge when they see Woe-is-Me coming.

Whether you went into hiding or sucked the life out of your peeps, your objective at this point should be to practice loving again. Think about some of the best relationships or friendships you have experienced. Who are your most loyal friends? What have you seen in other relationships that you've always wished you had? What specific qualities made those relationships stand out for you? Was it the communication? The level of trust? The belly laughs? The encouragement? What makes a relationship special? What elements of a relationship make you feel loved?

Once you've figured these out, commit to loving others in this way. Start with coworkers, neighbors, friends, and family. Start wherever you feel comfortable and expand to different groups of people until you've become a pro at loving others. If you know you appreciate it when people listen to you intently, or when someone genuinely asks how you are doing, practice doing these things for others. Then, take it a step further and ask your loved ones what makes *them* feel loved. Find out what puts a smile on their faces and do it!

This does two things. First, it gets you back into the rhythm of love. When you've got that rhythm, it's easier to love and trust, and people will find it easier to love and trust you. This process is gradual, yet may happen before you even realize it. The second benefit of practicing love is that you learn about the dynamics of love and how it works. You learn quite a bit about yourself—how you respond to different scenarios, whether or not you are as good at giving or receiving love as you thought you were, and how long it can take to build trust. You may even find that when you express your love, it is not always received as expected. There is much to learn about yourself and how you relate to love. You definitely won't learn it all as you practice loving others, but you certainly can learn some important lessons that you may be grateful you didn't have to learn within the context of a relationship. You then have the opportunity—in a safe environment—to make adjustments accordingly.

Rekindle Friendships

What's your social life looking like these days? Have you maintained strong relationships with your closest girlfriends? What about your male friends? If any of your friendships suffered during the time that you were in your relationship—or while you were recovering from it—now is a great time to rekindle some of those old bonds. Yes, this does sound a little like "crawling back" after things didn't go so well, but those friendships that are meant to last will carry on. Perhaps you can reexamine why those friendships lost their strength so that you can adjust how you maintain them next time you enter a relationship.

After my relationships with Jackson and Najee, I realized that I had an entire network of support all along that I had never tapped into. I had avoided some of these people because, quite honestly, they were truth tellers. They spoke truths that I was not ready or willing to accept. Other friendships struggled because one or both of us needed to pull away in order to stay on top of our complex lives. I reached out to both sets of people. With some, things just were not the same. We had grown apart. With others, I was blessed to develop a bond much deeper than anything we had experienced before. And a select few didn't respond at all. Some of my strongest friendships were developed and rekindled during this time, and the timing couldn't have been better. These rekindled friendships reminded me of what it felt like to have love and support in my life.

I had forgotten. I had forgotten what it meant to have someone close to me sit down and read my poetry (or anything I had written) and give me praise for it, as my parents had done when I was a child. I had forgotten what it was like to laugh hysterically over dinner with girlfriends. I had forgotten how freeing it was to just be me in the presence of those who loved me. No pressure. No expectations. Just me. I received an abundance of praise as a child, but by age thirty, the encouragement and compliments were few and far between. That is, until I developed and rekindled relationships with people who frequently encouraged me. That encouragement was powerful! It built a momentum in me that I hadn't seen since I was seventeen years old. It reminded me that I was loved and that my dreams meant something to someone outside of me. For the first time in years, I was surrounded by people who gave me a run-down of my strengths, simply because they wanted me to see what they saw. No strings attached. Just love.

If you spent a lot of time in an unhealthy relationship, you probably didn't get to hear these affirmations of your strengths either. This had become almost a foreign concept when I was married to Jackson. Living in a new city, working a new job in a toxic environment, and married to a guy who was more accustomed to receiving than giving compliments, my spirit and drive were being chipped away at slowly. I put out much more than I received. I had to learn all over again how to exist in a healthy relationship and what it felt like to live among people who loved me and actually expressed it.

Opening up was difficult at first because I didn't trust myself around well-intentioned people. I was deathly afraid of messing things up by talking too much, by not giving enough, by intimidating people, or by fully being myself. It took some time and a lot of practice to get used to being loved again—even by those who had been there all along. It was difficult to accept help because I feared that the offers weren't sincere or that I would suck the life out of this new support system. I wasn't used to having people on my team because I had shut so many people out for years.

No relationship should be so isolating that it snuffs out the very people who love you the most. I was blessed to have a support system that I didn't even know existed sitting right on the sidelines, ready to jump in after everything finally fell apart. They had no idea what I had been going through, but the timing of their reemergence into my life couldn't have been better. I'm so glad I was ready to receive them when I did! I was open and ready for a change—and they were right there to ride it out with me.

As you transition out of that old relationship, look around. You may be surprised to see who's been standing there all along with open arms, and who will emerge to take this new journey with you as you open up to new possibilities. It may be someone you've known your entire life, an acquaintance you never took the time to connect with, or someone you've been out of touch with for years.

Practice loving again by starting small and in safe territory—with those people who love you. Now is the time to relearn how to give and receive love. This is how you prepare yourself for a healthy, reciprocal relationship in which you have each other's backs and you support each other's dreams. These are the type of friendships you want to develop.

When you're ready for the real thing, you'll know what healthy feels like. You'll know how to give and receive love, and you will be far less likely to settle for anything less. Practice, practice,

practice—because what you do in practice, you'll repeat in the game.

Give love a little test run. Hopefully, you've committed to the journey of loving yourself. Now take it a step further and practice loving other people. Practice loving them the way you want to be loved, and then learn how to adjust to the way that they want to be loved. Are you ready? Go give it a shot.

Love you,

Dr. Pamela

Letter 35

THE DATING GAME

My Sister,

Embrace being single! This is your time to focus on *you* and to begin living your life to the fullest. This is not to say that you can't enjoy life while you're boo'd up, but your time as a single woman can lay the groundwork for how you'll live and enjoy your new life, regardless of whether you are single or in a relationship.

When I first became single again. I hated the idea of emerging into the world of dating. I was annoyed with the way men approached me, impatient with the process of meeting new people, and frustrated that I was a single woman in my mid-thirties. None of this had been according to the grand plan I had for my life. Eventually, though, I came to accept this new path. I found that dating had evolved into a whole different game than it had been the last time I was single. Twelve years earlier, before I had started dating Jackson, I was in my early twenties and in college. My dating pool was younger and more accessible. Everyone in my small college town seemed to know each other. Dating felt very safe. It also helped that I had a nice entourage of girlfriends who served as my sounding board and had my back whenever I met a new prospect.

As a single woman in my thirties, I was suddenly dating as a single mom with two kids in an entirely new age category (grown men in their thirties and forties), and in a new era (of internet dating in a hyper-sexed pop culture). The scene was hardly recognizable! The icing on the cake was that I was living in Atlanta—a city that allegedly has three times more single, eligible women than single, eligible men. The perception of this dynamic alone seemed to put women in a panic and compelled them to believe that they had to become much more aggressive than men. These women were much more tolerant of the variations of foolishness presented to them by the single, eligible men they chased. I had never lived in a major city before this, so Atlanta, complete with all of its reality TV-style baggage and drama, was quite the leap for me.

The first seven guys who approached me came with offers to spend the night at their houses—*that* night. I kid you not. We'd have a great conversation, complete with a few laughs, and then they'd pop the question: "Why don't you come to my house? I'll cook you breakfast in the morning." I admit, every time the offer was made, I was shocked and dumbfounded. But I'd play it cool and suggest a *different* type of first date—like dinner, perhaps. Or, oh I don't know...bowling? And I literally would never hear from the dude again. *Seriously?* I have since learned that many women would have jumped at such an offer. In fact, many would have made the offer themselves, which is why I was perceived to be a first class prude. So be it.

Instead of dating, I spent the entire first year in my new city focused on getting settled into my career (which is probably what I should have been doing in the first place). Other than the refreshingly occasional calls and visits from my still lingering, whatever-you-want-to-call-it "thing" with Najee (pre-Jamaica), I was pretty much dateless in Atlanta. I did meet one guy eventually, but he wasn't any more promising than those first seven "come spend the night and I'll cook you breakfast" encounters. We'll call him Zaire. We went out three times, and each date was progressively worse than the one before. It's an experience worth sharing.

Date #1

I met Zaire online after he somehow found me on Facebook and asked to connect with me. We didn't have any common friends, and I had never heard of this guy before. I hesitated at first. I don't typically connect with strangers online, but after two months of seeing his unanswered request sitting in my inbox, I decided, *What the heck? Why not?* We engaged in about six months of sporadic online conversation before I agreed to meet up with him for lunch. Zaire was extremely philosophical, which intrigued me at first. He expended a great deal of energy writing out and discussing his philosophical views on love, spirituality, the government, history, and social injustices. Though the topics he covered were not much different than those Najee and I often discussed, I wasn't feeling Zaire's vibe in the way I had with Najee. He just wasn't doing it for me. There was something unauthentic about this guy that I couldn't pinpoint.

After a nice lunch on the patio of an Asian fusion restaurant, Zaire caught me off guard when he asked me to drop him off at the bus stop, explaining that he had just been in a car accident a few weeks earlier and that he hasn't had a job for several months. Strikes *one* and *two*. The fact that he was going to need a ride back to his bus would've been great to know before the date. *But okay*, I thought, *let me just give this man the benefit of the doubt.* Why? Maybe because he was philosophical and I loved a good conversation. And let's just be real. I needed something to do.

Date #2

This time I decided to treat Zaire to my favorite restaurant for lunch—an elegant place with great, healthy food and amazing wine. In my year of solitude, I spent a lot of time exploring the city on my own. I experimented with restaurants and pampered myself with little in-town getaways (or staycations) at classy hotels that I managed to book at half-price on Hotwire.com. I chose a restaurant I loved next to one of my staycation hotels. Zaire was unfamiliar with the area, so the date started off with him getting lost. He was unable to find the restaurant on foot from the bus stop, which was just a block away. When he finally found the spot, he seemed shocked and out of his comfort zone. But he humored me and we engaged in another interesting session of conversation. This time around, I wasn't quite as fascinated, but I was very much curious about how he developed some of his far-fetched viewpoints. By now, I was tolerating him and his cynical philosophies on life, relationships, and the government (which he swore was watching him, even as we sat and talked over lunch). After that date, he wanted a kiss. I told him I wasn't ready.

Date #3

After I stomached date #2, I lost interest in carrying on conversations with Zaire. He'd call me and I would text back: *Hey, what's up?* He'd call me again, and I'd text him back again: *A little busy, but I can text.* I didn't want to have any more phone conversations with him, but I liked the idea of sharing a meal with someone after a year of dining alone, so we had one more date. I figured I could use the practice. This time, we went to a popular Chinese restaurant. That's when Zaire started to open up about his personal life. He told me that he was "technically" still married, but separated, that he "had to" put hands on his wife in front of their kids because she wouldn't stop "running her mouth", and that females in general are basically lost and clueless. Strikes *three, four,* and *five.* Married, abusive, and cynical. Wow, wow, and wow. I sat there, nodding and saying my "mmm hmms," wondering if he realized that this would be his last interaction with me. Ever. I didn't even bother to challenge or debate him because that would've kept us there longer. This just wasn't worth my time.

Once again, he asked for a kiss after walking me to my car, just before dashing off to his bus. I was shocked that he thought this was going somewhere. Again, I declined. Poor clueless guy. That was the last time I saw him. Out of curiosity, I did a web search on Zaire a few weeks later, only to find out that he was on multiple dating websites and discussion forums, looking for a *fifth* wife to go with his other four. Yes, that's right. Number five—as in Pamela and the four sister wives kicking it together in the same house, alternating intimate moments and bearing children with this unemployed philosopher. On one of the dating websites, Zaire went into great depth about the beauty of having numerous wives, and that his religion highly regarded this practice. Well, he sure as heck never mentioned *that* little tidbit of information during our three dates. Maybe he would've gotten to it by date ten.

But it only took three dates for me to see that Zaire was not a good fit for me by a long shot. He was:

✓ Financially unstable

✓ Abusive

✓ Cynical about women

✓ Religiously incompatible

Now let me be clear about the financially unstable thing. I don't want to sound materialistic and judgmental. I know the economy was a mess and a lot of people were losing jobs at this time. But here is my position. I worked very hard to get where I was. I had finally settled into the job of my dreams and had purchased a brand new five-bedroom home, just one month prior to our first date (and not for the purpose of housing Zaire and his four wives). I just exited a disappointing marriage, and I was finally on my feet. The absolute last thing I needed at that transitional point of my life was to take on a project, and especially one who had all of the extra baggage that Zaire was carrying. He talked a good game that fooled many into believing that he was a "deep" brother, but to just sit there and listen to what this man was actually saying revealed that this was nothing more than empty conspiracy theorist philosophy laced with big words and random, twisted facts that never went challenged. In his view, where he was in his life was everyone's fault but his own. I for one prefer a man who takes responsibility for his life.

It probably wasn't a horrible thing that I went on three dates with this dude, whom I sensed from the beginning wasn't my type. I went in with my eyes wide open and with a mindset that expected this to be an experience I could use as I reemerged into the world of dating. I considered it practice before the big game. I made my boundaries very clear and did not compromise. I was in control. No coming to my house (thank God). No kisses if I didn't want to. No trying to get him to like me. No fourth date if I didn't want one. I didn't go into it with relationship expectations. I wasn't set on finding my husband or even a new boyfriend. No sex buddies. No one-night stands. I just wanted to see what it meant to date these days and how I would handle myself. Did I really learn from my past relationships? Would I fall back into the same patterns? Was I strong enough to stick with the boundaries I had set for myself? I felt much more comfortable with the idea of dating when I approached it as *practice* and as a way of getting to know my new self. I wanted to see how this new me would interact with this new age group of men in a new era of dating. It was my own little personal research project.

I'll tell you, my sister, that year I took to focus on my career, to travel, and to pamper myself was dramatically life changing. It made all the difference when I started dating again. I was no longer dating as a needy person, but as a whole person. I no longer feared being alone, but grew to love my alone time. I no longer feared how people would perceive me because I was thoroughly pleased with the person I had become. I chose to surround myself with people who were also pleased with the person I had become. After Zaire, I chose to limit my dating options to people who were just as happy and fulfilled in their lives as I was.

Don't ask yourself if you *want* to date. Ask yourself if you are *ready*. Being ready means you have taken the time to truly refocus and rebuild. It means that you have done the following:

Refocus	Rebuild
With other people	Your self-esteem
Your priorities	Your strength
Your goals	Your ability to trust

If you have seriously taken the time to refocus and rebuild, then you may be ready to step back into the dating scene. In my next set of letters, I'll cover three different aspects of dating: the right and wrong reasons, defining your standards, and challenging yourself. In a nutshell, I recommend that you go into dating with a plan and some understanding of why you're doing what you're doing at all times. Make sense? Alright then, let's do this!

Love,

Dr. Pamela

Letter 36

THE RIGHT REASONS

My Sister,

For many of us, the first recourse after a breakup is to start dating as quickly as possible. Without a doubt, dating can be a great way to help us temporarily forget about the broken heart, but it can also cloud the healing process and perpetuate the problem. I cut my own healing process short by getting involved with Najee immediately after my divorce. As a result, I repeated some of my old behaviors and landed myself right back into another situation like the one I had just left. This is why it is so important to understand why that last relationship went south before you start putting yourself out there again. Taking your time helps you recognize old patterns that didn't work before and take measures not to fall into them again. Be patient and give yourself time before jumping into something else.

When Najee and I first started hanging out, I had no intentions of getting emotionally involved. I was just thrilled to have a new friend who listened and understood me. Because I wasn't paying attention, the unexpected chemistry between Najee and me quickly grew into a strong attraction for one another. He was some of what my ex-husband was not, and because of that, he just had to be *the one*. If you had asked me, I would've sworn up and down that I had been lucky enough to stumble out of one relationship and right into the arms of my long-awaited true love. *Um, no,* laughs my current self to my younger self.

Here's the thing. When you come out of a relationship in which there are a lot of deficits—a lack of faithfulness, affection, trust, or love—anyone (and I mean anyone) who can fill even one of those gaps will seem like that true love you've always wanted. This is because your focus right after a breakup is on what you didn't get out of that relationship. As soon as this new person is able to offer you that one very thing you didn't get from your ex, the rest of who they are almost doesn't matter. *So what that they are a free spirit who doesn't want to settle down and is totally emotionally unavailable? They listen to me and my ex did not. This has got to be the one!*

Girlfriend, at this point of your transition—right after the breakup—it is highly unlikely that your thinking is totally rational and clear. You may have to check yourself constantly to keep a level head. Most of us at this phase are living out of desperation. We want to make that pain go away. We want to be loved again. Desperation unaddressed does not result in a healthy you or a healthy relationship. It results in a desperate single life, and eventually, a desperate relationship on the rebound.

The Right Reasons to Date

Before you start dating, examine yourself. Are you truly ready? Is this a move of desperation? Do you understand why your last relationship ended and any role you may have played in its failure? Are you bitter? Afraid? Resentful? When you do step back out there, make sure you are doing so for the right reasons, and that you don't do anything too quickly. Here are a few right reasons to consider: to get to know yourself, to share your happiness, to have some fun, and because it's good practice. Dating is not supposed to be a dreadful task. It should not be approached as a desperate mission to find new love. Dating is an immersion into a social world that can be fun, fulfilling, and meaningful.

Reason #1: Get to Know Yourself

My dance with dating really didn't begin until after that not-so-romantic Jamaican cruise with Najee. That experience screamed loud and clear that he and I were not a match. Realizing that I had gotten involved with Najee much too soon after my divorce, I made it a point to give myself *time* before I started dating again. I'm not going to recommend any particular timeframe that you should follow. There really is no rule here. The amount of time you give yourself varies, depending on the situation—how long the relationship lasted, how intense the breakup was, and how much it disrupted your life. I was single and not dating for about a year after I moved to Atlanta. Most of that wasn't intentional—I was ready to date after about six months, but I was literally meeting a bunch of guys who only wanted nothing more than sexual relationships, which was incredibly frustrating. Rather than trying to shuffle through all the madness, I resolved that this was God's way of protecting me from something I wasn't ready for. Perhaps I still had more work to do—and I did.

The dating started slowly, with the first date in mid-July with Zaire the Philosopher, and the second in early September with a really nice guy I met at a restaurant and lounge downtown. But I had become immersed in rebuilding my life in this new city. My new priorities kept me busy and fulfilled. I had become a master of refocusing and rebuilding, so much so that I was in no great rush to fall in love again. Even with the slow start, I realized something very important about dating. It was an excellent way to get to know myself from a different angle.

I had grown so much after my last relationship. With a solid base of confidence, sexiness, and security, I found it fascinating to see how this new Pamela (and those new, smaller jeans) would fit in the dating world. Would I be able to recognize red flags? How would I respond when I saw them? Would I be as anxious as I was before to jump into a relationship? I wanted to know how this new me would respond to different guys in a variety of scenarios, and I was proud of myself! I loved this new sexy, confident, fun-loving girl! I knew what I wanted out of life, and I found that I had no problem sticking to my values and expectations with each new guy I met.

Many of them were eliminated from the first approach because they made their overly sexual, non-committal intentions very clear. I had grown to the point where I no longer set out to change anyone. I was able to nod my head and excuse myself from situations without looking back. "Oh, you aren't really into the church thing? That's cool." No judgment—but that was one of my cues to keep it moving. I knew what I did and did not want to welcome into my life. I had no reason to be so open-minded that I'd compromise my values. I was on top of the world and had nothing to lose by walking away from someone who couldn't guarantee to add rather than take away from my life. No longer was I the woman who expended incredible amounts of energy trying to mold someone into what I wanted him to be. He either was or was not. If he was not...next! It was that simple. I was quite proud of myself. This was great progress because it was the very thing I struggled with in my relationships with Brian, Jackson, and Najee. Through my era of dating, I learned a great deal about myself. When you do step out into the dating scene, pay attention. Put what you've learned into practice and get ready to introduce yourself to a new and amazing you.

Reason #2: Share Your Joy

Let me put this simply—if you're not joyous, don't date. If you're already miserable, dating will not bring joy to your life. This is part of the reason why the dating pool is as challenging as it is today. There are too many miserable, angry, and brokenhearted people in the mix. It serves yourself and everyone else well to stay out of the pool until you have healed. Please do not subject the world to your misery and despair. Your lack of joy is a sure sign that you've still got unfinished work to do. If that's where you are, it is not yet time to start dating. I once posted this message on Twitter:

If ur hurt & brokenhearted, don't jump into another relationship.
Chances are the person who hurt u was brokenhearted too.
#StopTheCycle

Think about it. By stepping out into the dating world as a hurt, brokenhearted, or bitter prospect for someone, you are asking them to welcome your pain into their lives. The likelihood that you will hurt them—or get hurt again yourself— is much higher than if the interaction involved two emotionally healthy people. Stop the cycle—don't get involved with people until you have recovered.

In a best-case scenario, dating would be for joyful people. When I started dating, I wanted to share that joy I had finally found in my life. Who doesn't want to date a joyful and secure person? A great time to start dating is after you have come to a place where you can truly say that you have a life of joy and are at peace with who you are. It makes the experience much more pleasurable. You'll more easily recognize the grump, the control freak, or the guy with low self-esteem. When you're joyful, you'll be less likely to hang around people who bring you down. You'll want to share your love and you'll find much fulfillment in doing so. Joyfully single is an excellent status to have when you get out there and start dating again. This makes dating less stressful and totally worth the wait.

Reason #3: Have Some Fun

A third reason to start dating is because it can be a lot of fun. Dating gives you the opportunity to meet new people and experience new things. One guy I briefly dated was also new to the city and had just committed to exploring the local fine dining. It was his mission to check out the city's finest restaurants and rate them. I had a similar mission, so we went to several restaurants we both had never visited. What a great collection of experiences! Being that I am a food lover, I had a blast. We eventually parted ways, but I came away with some great places to earmark for the future. Have fun with dating. Do something new like ice skating, painting, rock climbing, or attending an opera. Immerse yourself in the experience. In fact, focus more on the experience than the guy. You're not trying to find your mate right now. You're just trying to enjoy your life. The mate will come in time. For now, learn how to have a little fun without all of the strings attached.

Reason #4: It's Good Practice

When I first started dating again, I felt like I was dancing with two left feet. It was quite different from anything I had experienced as a young woman in my twenties. I quickly found that people were much more sexually free and that men and women didn't really seem to have much trust in one another anymore. I couldn't tell if these new developments were due to the new era or the new age group. Either way, I had a lot to learn and I decided to do that by practicing.

At the earliest phases of my reemergence into dating, I went out solely for the purpose of practicing. I started off with guys who seemed to be harmless—those overly humble and unintimidating types. I wasn't interested in something serious at the time, so I was very clear about the fact that I was fresh out of a serious relationship and was just looking to get out and have some fun. No pressure.

I have yet to meet a guy who isn't all for that. Guys actually seem to find the laid-back mentality quite refreshing—a woman who is easy-going and wants to enjoy life with no pressure and no games. The only challenge to that, however, is that some guys enjoyed my easy-going nature so much that they did eventually ask for something more serious. I had to stick to my guns until the timing and the situation were right. That sometimes meant having a difficult and awkward conversation, but this was all a part of my much needed growth process. I needed to become great at speaking up for myself—and I did. I also learned not to spend too much time with anyone I was not remotely interested in. What a great lesson in letting go and moving on when a situation didn't seem right. Practice it, and it will become easier over time.

There seems to be something about an easy-going woman that draws people to her as if they sense it, see it in her eyes, and smell it on her skin. I can't tell you how many men have told me that they were drawn to me specifically for that reason— because I seemed to be "cool" and they could just be themselves around me. When you're not taking the process too seriously— when you genuinely want to enjoy yourself and learn what you can—dating can be a great experience. It does come with its ups and downs, but ultimately, the experience is preparing you for the next phase of your life—learning to love again. It starts with baby steps, and before most babies take that first step, they crawl until they're strong enough and confident enough to walk. Your legs may be a little wobbly at first, like mine were, but give it a little time. You'll be dancing circles around the dance floor before you know it!

It's all in your approach. Just keep realistic expectations. You are in it to learn about yourself, to share your happiness, to have some fun, and to get some practice in. You don't have to worry about whether or not he's a dog or if he's lying to you or if you'll get hurt again. Your first dance with dating after heartbreak should never be that serious. Keep it light and enjoy yourself, but above all else, make sure you're ready.

Love you,

Dr. Pamela

Letter 37

DEFINE YOUR STANDARDS

My Sister,

When you start dating again, you'll get a lot of advice from family, friends, magazines, and TV shows. Some of that advice will be great and may resonate with you. Some will not. Here's *my* advice: decide what your standards are and use them as your guide. Your standards give you direction and keep you focused. As you date people with different personalities, interests, and careers, your standards should remain intact, changing only as you learn more about yourself and your needs. Your standards are a combination of your values, expectations, and desires. No one can define those for you. Everyone's standards are different, reflecting personal experiences, personalities, past relationships, and one's hopes and dreams for their lives. It's difficult to flesh out what your standards are if you haven't taken the time to think about who you are and what you've learned from your life experiences.

Upgrade the Checklist

When I was a young twenty-year-old in college, I thought I knew what I wanted in a man. My checklist was simple—someone who was educated, had a good job, loved his mother, and went to church. When I married this guy eight years later, I couldn't figure out what was missing. Jackson was *all* of those things. Life experience has since taught me that human beings are multidimensional and cannot be so simply categorized. As a researcher and professor of research, I have grown accustomed to asking deeper questions. What does educated mean, exactly? Educated how and to what extent? What makes a job good, and how will I recognize a good job when I see one? To go even deeper, how do these checklist items tell me who he is as a person? He's educated, but is he compassionate? He has a great job, but does he hate what he does every day? He adores his mother, but what is that relationship really like under the surface? And yes, he goes to church, but what is in his heart? I have since refined those young, idealistic, incomplete, non-specific checklist items to better reflect who I am as a woman.

Before I started dating again—after fifteen years of some real life experience—I sat down and thought about what my standards should be at this new phase of my life. This time, it wasn't just about the guy and what he would bring to the table. It was also about how compatible he was with me, how I felt in his presence, and whether or not he was receptive to what I brought to the table. My grown-up standards were a combination of the values, expectations, and desires that uniquely make up who I am. Checklists are about what the assets that they *have*. Standards are about *who* they are. It's time to upgrade that checklist and go deeper by defining your values, expectations, and desires.

Values

Your values are those core beliefs that give you conviction—the social causes you are passionate about, the spiritual beliefs you were raised with, the personal set of morals you abide by.

Your values keep you grounded. They make you care about the world around you. They are what make up your character and help shape your life purpose. When you define your standards, think about those values that you hold dear. Consider the role you want them to play in each of your relationships. Do they have to love animals? Would you prefer someone who is willing to pray with you? Must they be passionate about social justice? I personally value human dignity and social justice, so my guy must be aware of what's going on in the world around him and have a heart to improve the lives of others when he can. In the checklist I designed in my twenties, I specified that I wanted a man with "a good job." Understanding my values helped me to further define that to mean that I want a man who has a job that falls in line with his life purpose, because I highly value the idea of being in tune with one's purpose. Having a good job doesn't tell me much, but having a job that reflects his life purpose and values tells me a lot about who he is and how well he may fit with me.

Expectations

We all have very different expectations of ourselves and of the people we choose to date. Some women are so laid back, they just sort of shrug their shoulders with a "whatever happens, happens" sentiment. Others are so intense, they're calling off the date if doors are not opened for them. No judgment here. Your expectations are your own. I just want you to have some! Know your purpose for dating. Have an idea of how you expect to be treated. Define your limits—physically and emotionally. Decide early on what your limitations are for involving your kids in your dating life. I don't involve my kids at all in the early stages. I am very selective about whom I allow my kids to meet and what I tell them about my dating experiences. If it is not leading to a serious relationship that may result in marriage, they are not going to meet the guy, and they may never even hear about him.

If you just want to develop friendships and not pursue anything serious, be very clear about that to your dates and to yourself from the beginning. When you define your expectations, ask yourself what you want out of your experiences. Even if it is simply to have a good time, make sure you communicate that to the person you're. If you find that you're not having a good time—well, that's your cue to move on. Your combined expectations make a great measuring stick that can help you determine whether or not things are heading in the right direction.

Desires

Here's the part where you decide what qualities you want in your future partner and in your relationships. When I considered what it was that I desired in a man, I first thought about what I didn't have in my previous relationships that I longed to have. Three personality types rose to the top: a fun guy with a great sense of humor, someone who was intellectually stimulating enough to carry on a great conversation, and a guy who was highly supportive of my endeavors rather than intimidated by them. I knew that when I stepped back into another relationship, he had to have these qualities. To not have all three would be a deal-breaker, because these three qualities were directly compatible with whom I had become as a woman.

With such a clear picture of what I did and did not desire, it was very easy to know if someone I was dating would last very long. Above all, I desired to eventually fall in love and marry again, so I dated with this in mind. I didn't do one-night stands or spend too much time with anyone who fell short of my standards, because to do so would have been a distraction to my ultimate desire. There was no rush. I took my time, but I knew what I was out there for, and because of that, I stuck to my standards.

Did you notice how my grown-up standards differed dramatically from my original standards, which required only that he went to school, had a job, went to church, and loved his mama? I laugh when I think about that now, but I was so serious about my little checklist when I was twenty years old. I thought I was doing big things! Let me make a distinction between these set of standards and that checklist I once followed. Checklists are often shallow in nature. They consist of superficial qualities that can be checked off for the purpose of keeping or eliminating a prospect. Your standards, on the other hand, are not just about what the other person does or does not have or do. It is also about you. Your standards keep *you* in check. They keep you aware of whether or not you're moving in the right direction in terms of how you've defined your values, expectations, or desires. Are you compromising your values just to keep someone around? Are you merely tolerating them because they have money? Have you found that you are afraid to express your expectations? Have you decided that your desires don't really matter? If so, it's time to evaluate the situation. It may not be right for you.

Your standards are a reflection of who you are and the woman you have become as a result of experience and growth. No one can set those but you, but I'll tell you right now, people will have their opinions and will insert their unsolicited feedback. I've gone out with a couple of guys I wasn't feeling, and no one could understand why I didn't like them. One guy, for example was just gorgeous. Tall, beautiful lips, handsome, well dressed, and was crazy about me (he also loved his mama). He definitely would have met my checklist requirements, but he didn't meet my standards. He was insecure and was far from intellectually stimulating. Far, far, *far* away from it. Yet, he was sweet and a perfect gentleman. My friends thought I had lost my mind. "Girl, just date him and have your deep conversations with someone else!" they'd tell me.

But I just couldn't do it. I cut that one off within a few weeks. Another guy, seemingly perfect on the outside, admitted to having trust issues. I immediately left that scene. There was no fun in forcing myself to spend time with a guy who couldn't, at minimum, keep me interested on the date—or a guy who would be worried about my true whereabouts if I had to leave town to present at a conference (the thought of that alone makes me cringe).

When I first started dating again, I met some really great guys who were ready to settle down and get married, but I was far from wanting a serious relationship. I had just recovered from Najee, and wanted some air. I needed some space and time to enjoy my life as a single lady. I ultimately desired to be married, but during that phase of my life, I was still working on healing. My expectation at that time was to enjoy life. Settling would have been equally unfair to these guys because we all would have driven each other crazy. I had to stay true to my standards, and that saved everyone some grief.

The time I spent dating included a great collection of learning experiences. I learned much about myself and the value of my standards. I learned how to be honest with myself and how to stick to my guns. When you step out there, go out armed with a set of standards. They keep you in check and they help you focus on those people who best complement who you are. Make your dating experience one with no regrets and great times. It really is possible if you go out there with a purpose.

Love,

Dr. Pamela

♥ INSPIRE YOUR HEART

Take a second to consider your own standards. Jot down your values, expectations, and desires for dating in this new phase of your life.

Values	Desires	Expectations

Letter 38

CHALLENGE YOURSELF

My Sister,

Now the question on the table is how do you take that first step and start dating? These days, the options are endless with the dating websites, matchmaking services, singles groups, and social networking sites. I tried all of the above with great reluctance. I have to admit I wasn't necessarily thrilled about putting myself out there again, so I sort of tip-toed in with my back to the wall. I had no idea how to approach this dating thing as a newly single woman in my mid-thirties. It had been ten years since I last dated. All at once, I found myself in a new city, exploring this new era of dating in a much older age bracket than the one I had known in college. Suddenly, men in their forties with ex-wives and grown children were an option. I was scared out of my mind.

So, I started in the most distant and detached way possible—online. At the prompting of a few of my friends, I paid for a three-month membership and put up a half-hearted, incomplete profile. *Age thirty-four. Divorced. Two kids. Love to write.* Just the basics with a decent head shot. I didn't expect much. It was a start. But to my surprise, the moment I clicked "post," I started receiving messages. I mean, literally. Within the first few minutes, I had dinner invitations, compliments on my profile pic, and I even received some interesting photos that I had to instantly delete.

At first, it was flattering and fun, but after a couple of weeks, it became overwhelming and exhausting to go through profile after profile, deciding who I wanted to respond to and who should immediately be deleted. I engaged in brief, short-lived exchanges with the profiles on my screen, and then, because I was so filled with doubt and skepticism with the whole process, I'd lose interest. By the time my three months were up, I had met up with a grand total of *zero* guys. There were plenty of decent profiles to choose from. I just couldn't bring myself past the protective barrier of my computer screen. I felt safe in the comforts of my home. Perhaps I just wasn't ready, but it sure served as a nice fifty-nine dollar ego booster. I was a big hit online.

Don't get me wrong. I'm actually a huge supporter of online dating. I can see its benefits. Logically, it makes sense to search through profiles of people who have the very qualities you're looking for. Sure, online has its pitfalls, but so does meeting random guys in bars, grocery stores, and even church. Like with anything else, you have to trust your instincts and remember your standards. I have at least five friends who used an online service to meet the husbands they are currently married to. In fact, they are among the most happily married people I know. I can definitely see how online dating can work to bring compatible people together. I'm a fan. Give it a try. Don't be a big chicken like me.

I had a bit more success using common interest websites like Meetup.com because they create in-person and virtual social gatherings that allow participants to mingle and connect in non-threatening settings. Through Meetup, I joined singles groups that offered events like wine tasting, kayaking, hiking, and relationship discussions. I even felt confident enough to attend those events by myself, which seemed to increase my odds of meeting someone. I met a few guys this way, but I never went out with any of them more than once. No love connection. Still, this was the perfect way to get my feet wet and start practicing. I highly recommend group outings and legitimate websites like Meetup.com that host them.

The Ten-Date Challenge

I explored some great ways to get out there and date, but the single most successful strategy I tried was one that was presented on the *Tom Joyner Morning Show* by relationship expert, author, and TV host, Paul Brunson. I actually missed the show that morning, but I did what I often do when I wake up—check my phone to see what was going on in the social media world.

I saw a thread about the show on Twitter, inviting women to take on the challenge. *Challenge?* After further investigation, I learned that Brunson was a guest on the show that morning and had challenged women to ask ten men out by New Year's Eve. This ten-date challenge was designed to get us to step out of our comfort zones, to stop complaining about not being able to find a man, and to take charge of our own lives.

Given that I had absolutely nothing going on in the relationship department, I was immediately intrigued. I, who am not a morning person, popped up and did some quick laymen's calculations in my head. *I have sixty-one days at most. That's one new date every six days. Knock off a week between Christmas and New Year's because dates at those times are seen as "special" and I'm down to fifty-three days, which means a date every five days...I could totally do this!*

I had always been a bit more traditional and expected men to approach me. Like many other women, I was taught that I was the prize to be won and that I was to never initiate contact with a guy. I don't necessarily disagree with what I was taught, but that November morning, I sat up in my bed and decided to throw my inhibitions to the wind. I immediately tweeted a response to say that I was in. And so it began. During the months of November and December, I was on a mission to knock out this ten-date challenge.

The challenge changed my entire outlook on dating. Never in my life had I approached a man, but when I decided to do this challenge, I committed to throwing old ideas and fears out the window. What did I have to lose? If one said no, surely someone else would say yes. Right? I sure hoped so.

I have to admit I kind of cheated in the beginning. Just to warm myself up, I approached those guys who were least likely to turn me down. You know...the ones who already seemed to be somewhat interested or who seemed to be overly anxious to meet someone. I really was not at all interested in them, but I needed to get my confidence up. Horrible? Maybe... but it worked! After my first two dates, I was totally confident. I got flat-out creative with my approach by the time I got to guys three, four, and five. What I learned is that men are just as terrified, worried, self-conscious, and anxious as we are. They are just as human as we are. When we approach them or start the small-talk first, it's like they exhale! They're relieved and flattered. I was amazed to see how these guys went from playing it super cool to engaging in lively conversation when I approached them first. It was as if I had instantly thawed out that outer layer of ice. It wasn't long before I became a pro at covertly getting my mack on.

My best approach happened at one of my favorite bookstores. It was a Friday night, and my friend Crystal and I were there to chat and peruse some books in the café. She was excited that I was doing the challenge and insisted that I find my guy #3 that night. I personally was not really in mack mode, so I shrugged her off. As we sat there, flipping pages and chatting, she stopped in her tracks.

"Pam! That's the guy!" she whispered with an excitement that I was sure everyone in the café heard. "He just sat behind you, and he's really handsome. He's got pretty eyes—and oh my God! Look at that ring on his finger! You have to turn around and look."

"Crystal, I am not turning around."

"You have to ask him out! That's your guy #3!" Crystal went on and on about the man sitting behind me and his big blingy ring. I told her I was absolutely not going to approach a man wearing a wedding ring. She insisted that it wasn't a wedding ring—that it was something else that she couldn't quite make out.

"Quit staring," I whispered with a huge grin.

"Okay, I'm going to get up and go to the bathroom, and you are going to ask him out. Bye! Go do it!" and she was gone. Crystal left me there shaking my head and chuckling at her craziness. If this ring was big and flashy enough to catch her eye, I *really* wasn't interested. I wanted nothing to do with a guy who was more sparkly than I was. I like to keep it low-key.

But I was curious. So, I used that curiosity and a dose of honesty to approach this guy I had not yet turned around to look at. He was several tables behind me, so I had to actually get up and walk over to him. *Well here goes*, I thought. *Nothing to lose.*

I walked right over to him and smiled, "Hi." *Wow, he does have gorgeous eyes. Keep talking, Pam. Focus.* "I am so sorry to bother you, but my friend was going on and on about some ring you're wearing. I thought it would be really obvious and rude to turn all the way around to look, so I figured I'd just come over and ask you about it myself, if you don't mind. I'm Pam, by the way," and I stuck out my hand to firmly shake his.

He smiled and introduced himself. He explained that it was a Super Bowl ring and that he was a part of the winning team's physical therapy staff that year. *Ohhh...very cool. Wow. Look at that smile.*

He asked about the pile of books in my arms, and we ended up chatting it up until the bookstore closed. Crystal had been long gone by then. Gorgeous Eyes and I ended up exchanging numbers and met up for lunch that following Monday. And wouldn't you know it? He recommended my favorite restaurant—the very place I treated an uncomfortable, overly philosophical Zaire to just months earlier. The irony! And what a great date it was. We ended up sitting there for three hours sharing stories about our lives, our kids, and our dreams. It all started with my willingness to challenge myself, and an honest approach: *Let me see that ring.* Yes, I had become fearless. Brunson's ten-date challenge literally changed my life. By the time I knocked out the ten dates, my self-confidence and sense of power increased, and I landed an amazing relationship as a result of that experience.

Many women I've spoken to have asked: "How do you know if they really like you? How can you know if they would've pursued you if you were the one who asked him out?" My answer is: Trust me, honey! If he likes you, he will pursue you.

In fact, he may be so impressed with your confidence that he finds himself pursuing you even more. At least, that's what happened with the guys I approached. All it takes is breaking the ice. It could be as simple as a smile and a hello. The rest can be up to him if you want him to pick it up from there and take the lead. If he's not the kind of guy who would pursue a woman and prefers to lie back, well, he may *never* pursue you. If it's in his nature to do so, that brother will reverse those roles as soon as he gets his first opportunity—regardless of who made the first approach.

Challenge yourself. Do something that will stretch you as a person and will give you a whole new perspective. When I decided to do the ten-date challenge, I made it a point to do it without relationship expectations. My purpose was clear. I wanted to learn about myself and I wanted to have a good time. Missions accomplished—and then some! I met some great guys, went on some great dates, learned how to hold my head up high, and even found new love that exceeded my standards. Don't be afraid to put yourself out there and try something new. You never know what you'll find!

Love,

Dr. Pamela

CHAPTER TEN

RELOVING YOUR EX

Forgive them and release them over to God. Vengeance is mine sayeth the Lord. He knows how to compense you, rebuke them, and rebuild both of you.

\- Tera Carissa Hodges
Twitter Post, November 14, 2012

Letter 39

RELOVE *WHO?*

My Sister,

I know what you're thinking... *Relove my ex? Seriously?*

Yes, quite seriously! Don't worry. I haven't written you of these letters and taken you through this journey of healing only to advise you to go running back to your ex. It's actually quite the opposite.

You see, in my case (at least with regard to Brian and Jackson), I knew that I was going to be connected to my exes for the rest of my life. We each had a child together, so there was no walking away and dropping them from my life forever. How I envied those women who had the option to never, ever, ever, ever see their exes again—those women who could walk on and be that person their exes only *used* to know. I wasn't off the hook that easy. I had to learn how to coexist with these guys who had broken my heart. I had to be diplomatic. I had to do what I could on my end to make our necessary interactions bearable. Even if you didn't have a child with your ex, and even if you will never them again, you still have some work to do to ensure that your feelings toward them aren't resentful, because what you carry within you, you will carry right into your next situation.

I had to relove my exes so that I did not walk and live in resentment. When I say relove your ex, I mean discover a new way to love them. I'm talking about a human dignity type of love—a love-thy-neighbor type of love. You spent a period of your life loving them, and then perhaps hating them. Now it's time to learn how to love them all over again, but differently. Reloving was not something that I did for my exes. It was what I needed to do for myself. I needed to retain a spirit of love that protected my livelihood and my ability to function in their presence, no matter how they chose to act. I needed to keep my head together for myself and for the kids, and I needed to keep my heart together so that I would not be held back from embracing future love. This is precisely why you want to relove them. It doesn't matter if you will see that ex once a year, three times a week, or never again. You relove for your own peace of mind.

Now that the relationship is over, there are a few ways to solidify your healing and your ability to fully move on. First and foremost, forgiveness is your key to living (even if that just means forgiving yourself). I'll go into detail about this in my next letter, but if you have not forgiven, it's time to begin that process. Second, respect your ex as a human being. Whether or not you have to continue to interact with them, respect that ex and the role they once played in your life. Respect them in their presence and respect them behind their back. The third way to solidify your healing is to maintain an appreciation for the lessons you've learned as a result of your time together. If you've gone through all of this heartache and come out of it with a bitter chip on your shoulder, then you're going through this in vain, and you'll likely go through it again until you finally *get* it.

It's time to redefine their role in your life. Set your boundaries and establish a clear understanding of what they are to you today—not the one who got away or that person who did you wrong, but someone who taught you to find your voice or the person who is the parent of your child. This is how you come to a place of peace with them. Until you are at peace with the fact that the relationship is over, you will continue to carry baggage from this relationship to the next and to the next. The goal of reloving is to reach a point where talking about them, thinking about them, and even interacting with them no longer agitates a sore spot in your life.

This is especially important if the two of you have children together, but it is also important if you will never see them again. Why? Because learning to fill that gap with love, rather than with hate or resent is a very important key to your healing, your health, and your ability to move forward and love again. In my next set of letters, I'll share my final lessons and tell you how I learned how to relove those exes of mine.

Love,

Dr. Pamela

Letter 40

FORGIVE THEM

My Sister,

As I'm sure you know, it can take some time for all of that rawness to subside after a relationship ends. Even when the worst of it is over, many of us forget one final piece of moving on. We walk around with hard feelings and resentment for the ex, sometimes without even realizing it. If you harbor such feelings, it's important to understand how this affects you. Living this way eats away at your livelihood, your ability to trust, and ultimately, your ability to love again. Walking around upset with your ex does more to harm you than it does them. In fact, they may not even know that you're walking around with all of this hate, so it to carry that weight. Forgiveness and letting go is for you. This is not to do them a favor or to let them win. This is for *you*.

When Brian and I were together, he did some pretty horrible things. He threatened to kill me, pushed me to the ground when I was eight months pregnant, told everyone that our son wasn't his, and turned his back on me after I was sexually assaulted. Each of these would be considered highly unforgivable acts if you ask most people. It took me awhile to shake off the residue from that relationship, but as long as I held on, I continued to subject myself to the pain of it over and over again. I wanted him to apologize. I wanted him to see how horrible he had been to me and our son. I wanted him to come clean with it, and just finally say, "Pam, I'm sorry for everything I did to you." I wanted him to see how hard I tried to make the relationship work and keep the peace between us after it ended. I wanted credit for being a good girlfriend.

For years after we broke up, I entertained conversations with him about what went wrong in hopes that he would apologize. Most times, however, these "conversations" would turn into screaming matches of blame, and I would inevitably end up a hysterical ball of tears. Why the heck was this so important to me? What was I trying to prove in all of this? I didn't want him back. I had long moved on—or so I thought—and yet, I was determined to force this man to admit that he was wrong if it was the last thing I did. It was a ludicrous endeavor that I was never going to achieve because I was looking to the wrong person in my desperate pursuit of peace. It wasn't until I realized that I was in charge of my own peace that I stopped looking to Brian and began instead to look within for closure. The fact of the matter is that Brian was who he was. I could not change him and I could not change the past. I could only change myself. I had to forgive myself for subjecting myself to such an unhealthy relationship. I had to forgive him and let go of everything he did to me. It was over. I had to move on.

After our final screaming, snot-bawling episode over the phone, something awakened in me. I did nothing to this man and I knew it. My hands were clean. I decided that was the last time I would ever allow him to get me riled up that way. That was the last time he would ever make me cry. And it was. At that very moment, I decided to leave the pain of that relationship right there with him, and I walked away from it. That pain was not mine to carry because I had made peace with my own mistakes and could not—would not—take responsibility for his. Brian's actions and mindset were not for me to understand, rationalize, or sort out. It was my job to learn from this, forgive, and let go so that I could release myself from the past and spring forth into a more promising future.

I resolved that Brian was oblivious to the effect he had on me through the course of our relationship. He was heartbroken himself. He had a difficult upbringing and consequently treated me as he had been treated; he loved me as he had been loved. When I thought about it this way, I realized that his life was a very sad series of unresolved painful incidents that I chose to walk in on and embrace. Was what he did to me my fault? Absolutely not. Should he take responsibility? For sure! But ensuring that he did so was not my cross to bear. It was my responsibility to maintain my own integrity and to treat all people with love and respect, including Brian.

I had so completely released the pain, anger, and resentment that, years later when he actually did apologize, it added nothing to my life. I had long been healed. Grateful that he seemed to be progressing, I accepted the apology, but I continued on with my life as it had been before. This is what happens when you forgive truly. Your peace and happiness are not contingent upon what another person says or does. It's contingent upon what *you* say and do. You've got to find that peace within yourself, my sister.

I realize that forgiving is not easy for most of us. It's a learned skill that takes patience to master. The best way to approach forgiveness is to realize that you are doing this to relieve your mind, body, and soul of the stress and tension that keep you from truly relaxing. It relieves you from tensing up each time you hear their name. When you forgive, you take the burden off of your shoulders and allow yourself to walk, run, or dance forward with your life without the resentment of the past showing up to haunt you. If you struggle with forgiveness, try training yourself to adopt a forgiving mindset. There are several ways to do this: write it down, say it out loud, and keep things in perspective.

Write it Down

It may not surprise you that I find writing to be very therapeutic. I also find it to be quite empowering. Before I act upon a plan, I usually write down what I'm going to do. If I am preparing for a job interview or even a difficult conversation with a loved one, I take the time to think and write down my thoughts, questions, and concerns. I'm no different when it comes to preparing to forgive after someone has deeply hurt and disappointed me. It's nothing formal—just a statement to myself or to him about what was so hurtful, how it felt, and how I will no longer allow those feelings to have dominance or presence in my life.

I write about how my freedom comes with forgiveness and that on that very day, I will begin to shed all of the feelings of resentment that I feel as a result of that situation. I may not be there at that moment, but I write down where I *want* to be and what I want to feel when I am free from the burden of that situation. Then, I read that letter or statement as often as I need to as a reminder to myself of where I'm headed. I train my mind and my heart to forgive so that my body and attitude can follow suit.

I have also written short messages to myself on sticky notes—sometimes only one word—to encourage a spirit of forgiveness. I've hung the notes in random places like my bathroom mirror, my car steering wheel, my laptop, or the pantry—wherever I think it'll be useful to have a visual reminder. Before long, these messages have sunk in, and I eventually release the resentment, forgive, and move on with my life.

Say it Out Loud

Speaking your intentions out loud goes hand in hand with writing them down. You train your mind to forgive. What your mind hears, your body does. If you spend all of your time talking about how much you resent your ex, I can guarantee that you will be unnecessarily tense and unhappy. When you verbally declare to yourself that you forgive them, you set yourself up to believe it, even if you aren't quite there yet. Tell yourself that you are moving on with forgiveness because you love *you* and it's time to take charge of your life. Whatever you have to say, say it out loud—to yourself, to a trusted friend, even to your ex if you are ready for that. Say it out loud until that forgiveness becomes real.

Make it a point to keep it positive. Everything you speak and hear should propel you into the direction of forgiveness. Surround yourself with people who speak positively and in an uplifting manner, rather than those who encourage you to bad mouth him, thereby helping to keep you in a negative state of mind. When people attempt to speak negatively about your ex, tell them that you have moved on to a new and higher level in your life and that you are choosing not to bring yourself down with the negative talk. If they can't respect that, then kindly avoid further conversations with them about your ex. This is your life. Insist on handling it with strength and integrity by speaking only words of strength and integrity. What you speak is what you become.

Pray About It

Sometimes people don't forgive because they don't want to. You may not have a desire to forgive your ex at this time. You may enjoy hating on them and talking trash because it feels like a good release. It *can* feel like a good release at first—when the situation is still fresh. But after awhile, it's time to let that baggage go. If you find that you have no desire to forgive, you may need to reach outside of yourself and pray for that desire. Pray for the ability. Pray for peace in your heart. Forgiveness is a spiritual process. It challenges you to look beyond the nastiness of what you're feeling today and into a future where you see yourself free.

Doing something as highly spiritual as forgiving takes effort that doesn't always come naturally. Total forgiveness is still a work in progress for me. Rarely, but every now and then, an interaction with one of my exes triggers emotions of anger that I didn't realize were still there. I'm human. It happens, but I make it a point to recognize those moments and to keep my emotions under control. Over time, I've noticed great improvement because I have made forgiveness a priority. Prayer has helped me go beyond my comfort zone. It enables me to do what I never thought was possible or what I may have no desire to do. Pray about it, but also be proactive. Go through the motions of forgiveness by writing it down and speaking it out until you finally begin to experience a shift in your heart. For some, it may happen right away. For others, it can take awhile. Be patient with yourself and trust that in time, your change will come. You will develop the ability to forgive if you stay disciplined and train yourself to take that step.

Keep Things in Perspective

Please remember to keep things in perspective. Remember why you are forgiving: to bring peace to your life and to claim the ability to love wholly again. You are not doing this to get a reaction out of your ex. You are not forgiving with hopes that they will apologize or see you as a better person. Be realistic with yourself about what you are able to do. Everyone's process is different and happens in different timeframes. As long as you make a sincere effort to forgive and move forward with your life, you will make progress at your own pace. Get creative. Toy with some strategies and find out what works for you. If necessary, connect with a life coach who can help you with a strategy. Having someone who can hold you accountable for something that is difficult to do makes all the difference in the world.

Where do you stand on forgiveness? If you have even a tinge of bitterness resting on your shoulders, you still have some forgiving to do. Forgive so you can relove.

Love,

Dr. Pamela

Letter 41

RESPECT YOUR EX

My Sister,

In the midst of the bitter breakups with Brian and Jackson, I made a conscious choice to never treat either one of them disrespectfully. We each had a child together and I wanted to be fair to my son and my daughter. I made it a point to never speak negatively to or about their fathers so that their relationships would not be tainted by my experiences with them.

Now, just because I made the decision to maintain dignity and respect does not mean that they did the same, and it definitely doesn't mean that this was easy. Both Brian and Jackson were highly disrespectful to me. For a time, they each tried to push my buttons to get a rise out of me. I stuck to my guns, choosing to pray under my breath rather than curse them out, or to sit down and write rather than to slash some tires. Trust me, it was not easy to keep my cool, but I knew that responding in anger or retaliating would have invoked an all-out war—a war that they were each more than ready to engage in.

I'm not asking you to become your ex's doormat and to not stand up for yourself. By all means, respond to the foolishness. Just be wise in your approach. Keep your responses dignified. When Jackson threatened to take custody of our daughter after I landed my dream job in Atlanta, I kept my cool. I calmly asked him to think about what would be best for her. But when I left his presence freaked out and angry, I cried and prayed desperately. I knew that acting a fool in front of him would only fuel his vengeance, so I had to play it cool. I didn't just pray for myself. He was hurt and brokenhearted from the divorce, so I prayed for peace in his heart. I prayed for wisdom, and I prayed that all would work out in the best interests of our daughter.

Within a few weeks, Jackson agreed to transfer his job to Atlanta so that our daughter would have both of us within her reach. His transfer process was fairly easy because the company he worked for had many branches in the Atlanta area. It was more a matter of his choosing to initiate that process. Had I decided to go off on him and hire a lawyer in anger, I would've had a fight on my hands—one that our daughter would have surely lost. Because I remained prayerful and peaceful and never wavered in my respect for Jackson, he was much more willing to work with me than against me for the sake of our daughter. There was nothing passive about my behavior; I actually was quite assertive, encouraging him to transfer, offering to discuss options that would benefit our daughter, doing some legal research on the side (because you always want to be prepared), and staying prayerful by the minute. I am so grateful that Jackson had a change of heart and chose to put our daughter's needs first.

Brian wasn't quite so easy to work with. He was so hot-tempered and unpredictable, I just removed myself from his presence altogether. For a while, he lived only twenty minutes from my son and I but would not call or show much interest in being involved. Rather than give the man hell and try to force him to do anything, I stayed out of his way, but I was always accessible so that he could reach out to his son if he wanted to.

Never did I volunteer my presence. I was in grad school and working full time, so if I needed a babysitter or if I was short on funds, I found ways to make it happen by getting a roommate to help with expenses, by asking a classmate to babysit, or by bringing my son to class with me. I operated as if Brian didn't exist. It was easier to do that than to stress myself out trying to make him do something he refused to do. It wasn't worth it to call and beg him to help out with his son. Child support was court-ordered, so at the very least, I received a couple hundred every month. Anything I needed above and beyond that wasn't worth the fight. When Brian did come around, I didn't roll my eyes or give him the cold shoulder or attempt to tell him about himself. I learned to grit my teeth with a smile as I watched my ecstatic six-year-old run and jump into his dad's arms. All the while, I'm saying prayers under my breath (not swears, but prayers), and making it a point to treat the man with respect. The last thing my son needed to see was his mom tearing into his dad during what he perceived to be a happy reunion. My child would have never understood such anger at his young and tender age.

What I discovered is that my dignity and respect set the tone for how these post breakup relationships unfolded. If I had a nasty attitude, the guys would follow suit. If I had responded dramatically to their drama, my life would have been a soap opera nightmare to this very day. My decision to respond with respect squelched the fire—maybe not right away, but they certainly had no ammunition to keep the fire going. Though it took Brian much longer to chill out, he eventually realized that the best way to work with me was to work *with* me. I was above the drama and well past crumbling into a well of tears when either Jackson or Brian got upset or frustrated with me. If I felt so overwhelmed that I wanted to cry, it was no longer in front of

them. What they got when they saw me was a wall of strength—
a wall that they eventually realized could no longer be
penetrated. I was the epitome of self-control. As a result, I had
control over the situation. My interactions with them emanated
a very clear message: *I've got no time or energy to spend on
drama. You are a part of my past, and I've got other things I'm
focused on these days. So let's take care of our children and keep it
moving.* They got the message, and for that, I am grateful.

My sister, you have a lot of power. Don't be the initiator of
drama, and don't accept any drama. Respect your ex as an
important piece of your past—the piece that is helping you
evolve into the woman you are becoming. If they are a parent of
your child, respect them as such. The one who loves and
respects is the dominant one and truly leads the way. You set
the tone. You have the power. Stick to your guns and live your
life in peace.

Love you,

Dr. Pamela

Letter 42

EMBRACE THE LESSONS

My Sister,

Now that the dust has settled, I have grown to appreciate my exes for teaching me some vitally important lessons that I was too hard-headed to learn before each of them crossed my path. Life lessons are interesting in that they continue to present themselves with increased intensity until we finally wake up and start to do things differently. Here's a simple example to illustrate what I mean. When I first met Brian, my instincts told me he wasn't right. In fact, they were screaming at me. I didn't listen. Then my parents told me. I didn't listen—but I was nineteen and I sure as heck didn't want to listen to them. Then my friends told me. In fact, many of them dismissed themselves from my life as his actions grew increasingly erratic.

One such friend, for example, lived in the same apartment complex that Brian lived in across town. On this particular day, Brian and I were on the phone, at it again. Fighting. I was trying to convince him that the baby I was carrying was indeed his child, and that he was the only guy I had ever been with. Ever. He suddenly flipped out on me, accused me of lying, and threatened to kill himself. Once again, instead of this being my sob story, he was going to make it his. The old reverse psychology trick. "I have a pencil in my hand, Pam, and I am about to stab myself in the neck."

He knew me well because he got exactly the reaction he wanted. I panicked. I became hysterical, begging him not to end his life. I could picture the scene he described vividly, and the images of Brian doing this horrible thing freaked me out. I begged and cried until I suddenly heard a choking noise. He had done it! When he wouldn't respond to me, I immediately hung up the phone and called my friend, Shauna, frantically trying to explain what had just happened. She called 9-1-1 and ran over to his apartment. He wouldn't answer the door for her, but when the ambulance arrived, Brian flung the door open in a rage, unharmed, cursing everyone out—the emergency crew, his neighbors, and Shauna. He had not stabbed himself in the neck. After that episode, Shauna told me that she wanted no part of this drama in my life and asked me never to call her again. In honor of her request, we haven't spoken since.

Was that enough to make me get up and walk away from Brian? No. That was only the beginning! That was our honeymoon phase. I waited an entire year and a half *after* that before I decided to do things differently. I was hard-headed. I was pregnant by this guy, so it was my self-proclaimed mission to get him right and make this lopsided relationship work. I did learn eventually. Though the journey was rough, I am grateful for the very important lessons learned. I can't regret them. I can't despise Brian for coming into my life, because I did it. I allowed him in and I allowed him to stay long enough to take what I needed from the experience.

One vital part of the healing process is to embrace the lessons that were borne out of your experience in that relationship. Your takeaway from the situation is not about what they did or did not do, but about how you will live your life from here on out. It's about looking at who you've become and deciding where you need to go from here. If you don't take note of the lessons learned, I can guarantee that you will not grow from where you were and you may continue to find yourself in similar situations in the future. Don't let that experience be one that you endured in vain.

As I look back and think about what I learned from my experiences with Brian, Jackson, and Najee, a pattern is crystal clear. I didn't listen to what they were telling me and what they were showing me. In all three situations, I wanted to get married. I wanted affection. I wanted a whirlwind romance. And in all three situations, they did not. For each of their own reasons, they were not ready. But I am a take-control-of-my-life kind of girl, so I was just going to *make* it happen, come hell or high water. In my quest to take control, I had actually lost all control. My grasp of reality was gone. I was determined to convince them to love me and to go along with me into my dreams of a fairytale romance—even while I was dragging them in kicking and screaming. That's the overarching theme, but of course, it played out much differently with each relationship.

Brian

When I met Brian, I was eighteen years old. He was twenty-four and had just broken off an engagement with a fiancée who cheated on him. By his account, he caught her in the very act of sleeping with this other man. The fact that I met him only months after this devastating life event should have been a blazing red flag, but I was eighteen and he was the first guy I ever dated. What did I know about rebounds, heartbreaks, and baggage? Nada. I was totally clueless. He came to me broken, closed up, and afraid to trust, sure that I was likely to do to him what his ex had done. Even in my cluelessness about rebounds, heartbreaks, and baggage, there were plenty of other signs to make note of—signs that I saw and blatantly ignored.

Brian's living situation was questionable and didn't match the lifestyle of the job he claimed to have. When I met him, he told me that he was a police officer. But he—a twenty-four-year-old man— lived in an overcrowded house in the worst part of town with his able-bodied mother, her shifty husband, and the slew of grandkids she inherited from her drug-addicted daughter so that she could get a government check. Nothing fishy there, Pam?

I soon discovered that Brian was not a police officer, but a Walmart security guard. I'm not knocking the profession. I'm just saying...that blatant lie should have sent me running to the hills. But I didn't run. I was on a mission to get him saved and married. Over the next year and a half, the lies, the signs, the fear, and the abuse snowballed. I had become so used to ignoring it all that I was in deep before I realized what I had gotten myself into.

But what's done is done. The most important thing is that I learned greatly from this experience. In my period of rebuilding, I forgave myself for accepting all of that drama into my life. I forgave myself for ignoring everything and plowing forward to get what I wanted. I forgave myself for the fear of single motherhood that lead to my marriage obsession and my blatant refusal to look at what was standing in front of me. The irony in all of this? I ended up a single mom anyway, and once I embraced being a single mom, it actually wasn't such a terrible thing after all. Single motherhood was the very thing, in fact, that helped me find my wings in life. I worked so hard because my son inspired me to. He kept me motivated to finish college, to buy a house, and to go to grad school. Marrying Brian would have yielded exactly the opposite results.

✓ Lesson Learned

Jackson

Jackson is a good guy with a good heart. He had just come out of a three-year relationship with his first love—a beautiful young lady who had relocated to a different state for college and broke up with him before leaving. Sure that he was going to marry her, Jackson was devastated. After that situation, he resolved never again to open up to another woman the way that he had with his ex. By the time Jackson and I met, he, like Brian, was on the rebound. And once again, I showed up just in time to be his rebound girl. Jackson was so great with his little sister, my young son, his developmentally delayed clients, his mother, and his grandmother that it didn't matter that he wasn't so great with me. Who cares that he had built a wall to keep me out? I resolved that I would love Jackson with a strength powerful enough to break down that wall. I would get him into church and get him saved. Sound familiar? I kid you not. This was my mission—once again. It was as if I had no memory of what I had just walked away from almost exactly one year earlier. Though a year had passed, I had never taken the time to recognize patterns in my own behavior. I was in the prime of my college years while raising a son. Evaluating patterns of behavior was a foreign concept to me.

Still oblivious to the concept of baggage and rebounds, I didn't understand why Jackson wouldn't open up to me. The longer I waited, the more accustomed he became to being closed to me—because my being there told him that his behavior was okay. This remained the tone of our entire eleven-year on again, off again relationship. I was on another marriage mission for the exact same reasons. I wanted a father for my son. I wanted the happy, complete family. So, I accepted whatever I could get from Jackson, content with living my life behind his wall.

✓   Lesson Learned

Najee

My friendship with Najee was not necessarily a negative one, but it definitely became strained as I (once again) attempted to push him into something he wasn't interested in having. I wasn't listening to what he had very clearly telling been me all along. His priority was not to nurture a romantic relationship. He was fully committed to his music and work in the arts. In a situation like that where we had a great affinity for one another, but very different motives for our lives and each other, I needed to stop and listen. Instead of hanging around hoping, praying, and waiting for him to change his mind, I would have served myself well by accepting his friendship as just that—a friendship. Move on. Keep dating. Don't stop enjoying life. If Najee and I were not on the same page, there never should have been a tug-of-war. The fact of the matter is I don't want a man I have to rope into my life. I desire a relationship in which both parties are excited and willing. If that's what I desire and if that's what I believe I deserve, I need to put the ropes away and let my Mr. Right come on his own—a Mr. Right who meets my values, expectations, *and* desires. Najee and I had mismatched expectations. Had I been following my standards, I would have recognized our incompatibility right away.

✓   Lesson Learned

This lesson learning stuff can be a humbling process, but it's absolutely necessary to make note of those lessons learned and to have an appreciation for your ex's role in that process. No one wants to think about some of the foolish things they may have done in past relationships, but we have all been there in one way or another. Even my parents who have been happily married for thirty-eight years can look back and reflect upon some lessons they've learned from each other. And they're still together. Surely there are some lessons you can glean from past relationships that *didn't* last. You never know who's looking up to you and who can learn from your experiences. Your life lessons may very well serve to help others who are struggling in their own relationships. What have you learned about yourself through the course of your relationships? Are there any patterns? What has been your consistent weakness? How will you resolve that issue? The sooner and more diligently you pursue answers to these questions, the less likely you will be to walk these same patterns of behavior and thinking into your next relationship.

Love you,

Dr. Pamela

♥   Inspire Your Heart

---

1. What are the most important lessons I learned in my last relationship?

2. What did I learn about myself?

3. What patterns do I see in my life that need to stop?

4. What will I do differently from now on?

Letter 43

REDEFINE THEIR ROLE IN YOUR LIFE

My Sister,

All three of my exes are still in my life—two because we have children together, and one because we are good friends. In each case, I had to redefine the relationship and be very clear to them and to myself about what their roles in my life would be. One thing I've noticed about each of them is that they were all quite excellent at drawing the line in the sand and sticking with their boundaries when we were together. When Brian didn't want to talk to me, he didn't answer the phone. When Najee said no relationship, he made it a point not to let us get too close. And when Jackson said he wasn't opening up to any other woman, he erected a wall to protect his heart from me. On top of that, all three of them limited my access to their families, friends, and personal lives.

I, on the other hand, was an open book. I established no clear boundaries and no standards to which I held. They each had an all-access pass to my life well before that pass was earned, so when it was time to redefine their roles in my life, I took a lesson from each of them and drew my own lines in the sand.

I borrowed from their strategies—not necessarily by erecting a wall to keep love out, but by redefining physical and emotional boundaries, and by ensuring that I would no longer be vulnerable to them in this new phase of my life. I knew that I was not going to be getting back with these guys, so I made it a point to set boundaries and redefine each of their roles. My relationship with Brian was flat-out toxic. Jackson and I were incompatible. Najee's life objectives clashed with my own. Once I fully acknowledged these truths, there was no more dancing around the possibilities. It was over, over, and over. We were all best served to move on with our lives.

One clear difference I noticed between my exes and myself is how we compartmentalized our lives. They each seemed to have a special place for everything. The girlfriend goes here, the kids go there, the sports are over there, and work goes up there. With me, there was no compartmentalizing. Everything just sort of ran together. I introduced one part of my life to another and multitasked so that I was mixing work with motherhood with dating with leisure. I did this—and then got frustrated when the guy in my life refused to do the same. At some point, I had to step back for a second and consider this scenario. They were doing something I was not. They were setting boundaries, defining limits, drawing their lines in the sand. They said no when I wanted to infringe upon their work lives, their fatherhood, and their leisure time before they were ready to let me in. This is precisely what I needed to do—with my exes, with people I dated, with anyone who asked to cross my boundaries. When I finally realized this, I made it a point to take my boundaries more seriously.

Makeup/breakup cycles happen when boundaries are not set or enforced. Consider these scenarios:

- Your ex comes over to drop off the kids. They make a flirtatious comment. You love it. Boundaries and everything else drop to the floor.

- You're dating someone new. Your ex doesn't like it. The ex interrogates you about your life and makes sarcastic comments about this new person. You begin to confide in your ex about the new relationship.

- Your ex has fallen on some hard times and asks if they can stay with you until they gets back on their feet. You agree to let them stay—just until they get it together.

- Your ex buys you expensive gifts for your birthday and holidays with hopes that you'll take them back. You accept the gifts because they've never done anything like that for you before, and after all that crap you put up with when you were together, you deserve this!

All of these scenarios demonstrate a failure to establish clear and firm boundaries. Without boundaries, contact with the ex can become a slippery slope. You may do something you regret, have them in your personal business and personal space, or find yourself feeling obligated to entertain them. Cut the strings. Decide what is acceptable and make your boundaries very clear to them. They may test those boundaries a few times, but if you stick to your guns, they'll get the message. But let's not put this all on your ex. Truth be told, you may be tempted to cross those lines yourself. This is precisely why you want to develop those boundaries and remind yourself regularly how important it is to stick with them.

There is no universal set of boundaries. Your boundaries will depend on the nature of the relationship, the dynamics of the break-up, and what you feel comfortable with as you move forward.

The boundaries I set for Brian, Jackson, and Najee were as different as each of our relationships. My boundaries became the basis for how each of our new relationships were to be defined. In most cases, if you treat them with respect, but make it very clear where they now stand in your life, they will respect you and their new roles, even if not right away. Be patient with the process. It will happen. As with most other transformations, this doesn't happen over night. It takes time for the two of you to adapt. Just be sure that you stick to your guns. Keep your boundaries sacred. You are single. This is your life, my sister. Run it as you see fit!

Love you,

Dr. Pamela

♥ INSPIRE YOUR HEART

1. Am I comfortable with a friendship, or do I prefer that my ex remains a distant acquaintance?

2. What are my weaknesses when it comes to my ex?

3. What areas of my life will my ex have access to? What is no longer accessible?

4. What rules do I need to set to ensure that my boundaries are not crossed?

5. Do I feel threatened by my ex? If so, what type of help can I seek to alleviate that threat?

Letter 44

FINAL THOUGHTS:
IT'S YOUR LIFE... LOVE IT!

My Beautiful Sister,

You made it! I hope that this has been a therapeutic, empowering, and comforting process for you. I know that your journey has only just begun. The fact that you've made it this far speaks volumes. You're serious about your healing! I commend you for that. Just remember to take the time to refocus, rebuild, and relove before you jump into another relationship. This is so important because these phases—especially refocusing and rebuilding—help you to stand on your own two feet, to move through the tears, and to mend what is broken. Move at your own pace. If you have to go back and revisit some letters, do that as often as you need to.

It was through my own series of experiences—my journey—that I learned to truly love my life. I didn't fully understand what it meant to heal after the ending of a relationship, so I stumbled along until I finally figured it out. I am grateful to finally receive all that I have anticipated through my healing process. I am grateful for what I have in my life today. Regardless of what the future holds and who will hold me in the future, it only gets better from here. There's no going back to where I was before! I know too much about what's possible to ever again let myself deteriorate over a failed relationship.

Remember, my sister, this is your life. You are the artist. You have the power to take that clay in your hands and mold it into whatever you like. You can take any broken pieces and use the gold deep within you to create something new. You have the power to walk in peace and happiness. You have the liberty to dance in the dark, on the streets, in the comforts of your living room, in front of strangers, hand in hand with your children, and eventually with the new love of your life. When you truly understand this, when your heart burns with passion again—this time, *for yourself*—nothing, my sister, will be able to stop you. Not even a broken heart. It's your life—love it and live it well!

Love you much,

Dr. Pamela